TABLE OF CONTENTS

WRITING
FROM WITHIN

"Very deep . . .
very deep is the well
of the past."

Thomas Mann
Joseph and His Brothers

Other books and films by Bernard Selling:

Writing From Within: A Teaching Guide
Best Autobiographical Stories from Life-writing Classes
The Flying Machine (from a story by Ray Bradbury)
Three Miraculous Soldiers (from a story by Stephen Crane)
First Year A.D.
Little Train
Henry

Writing
From
Within

A Step-by-Step Guide
to Writing Your Life's Stories

◊ ◊ ◊ ◊ ◊

BERNARD SELLING

First U.S. paperback edition published in 1989 by Hunter House Inc.

First U.S. classroom edition published in 1988 by Hunter House Inc.

Hunter House Inc., Publishers
P.O. Box 847
Claremont, CA 91711

Library of Congress Cataloging-in-Publication Data

Selling, Bernard.
    Writing from within.

    Bibliography: p. 236
    1. Autobiography. 2. United States—Biography.
I. Title.
CT25.S45   1989   920'.073   88-755
ISBN 0-89793-052-5 (classroom edition)
ISBN 0-89793-054-1 (paperback edition)
ISBN 0-89793-061-1 (cloth edition)

Book design by Furbeyre & Associates
Cover design by Teri Robertson
Copy editing by Kiran S. Rana
Production by Paul J. Frindt
Set in 11 on 13 point Century Schoolbook by
    847 Communications, Claremont, CA
Printed by Edwards Brothers, Inc., Ann Arbor, MI
Manufactured in the United States of America

9 8 7 6 5 4 3 2 1   First edition

PREFACE

WHEN I WAS SIXTEEN YEARS OLD, MY FATHER died—an unexpected and sad event for me. He was an enigma: a prominent psychiatrist, the possessor of seven college degrees; an angry and charming man, highly ethical, overbearing, and accomplished. A heart attack eight years before his death caused him to stumble toward the finish line of his life like an exhausted marathon runner whose sole purpose in life was to achieve his own personal goal: to stay alive until his children finished high school. He almost made it. For weeks after his death, I read copies of all the letters he wrote during his years of public life. Nowhere could I find anything personal about him: who he was, where he had come from, where he thought he was going.

Beyond a few facts and remembrances and a few funny stories, I knew very little. My mother died a few years after my father and I reached young adulthood in the 1950s feeling like an existential antihero—free to make choices but not guided by an immediate past or a family history—truly alone.

In the intervening years, from Dad's death until the present, my father's sister, the one person who could reveal more of him, showed no interest in telling me more of his early life.

"People of our generation do not dwell on such things," she would say. "I don't have time." So it appeared that my father's history, both family and personal, would remain shrouded in darkness, consigned to oblivion. And indeed it has come to pass. This has saddened me enormously.

When asked to teach the classes from which this book was drawn, I thought how much it would have meant to me to know my parents well: how they were raised, the things they did, and most of all, what they thought and felt as they experienced their lives. This became my touchstone for teaching the class—actions and events accurately described, feelings about them honestly and vividly captured.

As the classes developed over several years, I began to realize the importance of what we were accomplishing.

First of all, the writing process was immensely therapeutic for each person. It was plain to see that once the participants had overcome a fear of writing, the process of getting their life histories out and on paper had a revitalizing effect on them.

Second, the process of being congratulated for good work and encouraged by class members to keep at the task was equally therapeutic and informative.

Third, the warm acceptance of their work by family members revealed to each person that he or she was filling a genuine need within the family.

Fourth, and most inspiring, was the awareness that, as each writer became more skilled, the quality of his or her legacy would itself become a touchstone for the family and inspire histories to be written by generations yet unborn. Occasionally, someone would comment after a particularly good story, "What would it be like for us if our parents and forebears had left memories as well-written and revealing as the stories which are coming to the surface in our workshop?"

Ultimately, this is the great lure of life-story writing: to be able to affect the future of the families into which we are born; to give direction, amusement, and perspective to our children's children and their children; to write so well that a hundred years from now those who follow can clearly see the footprints which we made, and can begin to gauge their own paths by our direction.

I would like to thank Betty Springer and Gyl Roland for their support, advice, and encouragement, and Ruth Tachna for her editorial assistance with this volume. I would of course like to thank the students in my life-story classes, without whom this volume could not have been written. To Jack Garfein, who heads the Actors and Directors Lab in Los Angeles and New York, I must also express my gratitude, for it was in his acting, directing, and writing classes that I learned the Stanislavski approach to drama, an approach which has inspired many of the techniques I use in my writing classes.

Bernard Selling
Venice, California, 1989

To Lowell and Mary,
my parents

INTRODUCTION

FOR MANY YEARS, OBSERVERS OF AMERICAN culture—David Riesman, Alvin Toffler, and others—have noted the rootlessness and materialism of our society as well as its loosening connections to its own past, and they have examined with care the catalysts of this rootlessness, the upwardly mobile American middle-class. None of these observers, however, paid enough attention to the patterns of life of those left behind: parents and grandparents.

But over the past ten years, we have seen a distinct shift toward respect for roots. And with it, an increasing respect for the wit and wisdom of those who have brought us to where we are—those same parents and grandparents. For a writer and teacher who works with mature adults, this is a welcome change.

This volume is written for those who wish to inform their children and grandchildren about the life path which they, the writers, have followed. It is a self-help text, derived from the life-history writing classes I have been teaching in Los Angeles, California.

The book is in three parts. Part I exposes the writer to various techniques which will help him learn to express himself fully and well on paper (—or "her... herself"—till our language finds a good word that includes both sexes, we writers have to make certain choices. The use of he, him, etc. in the text is a convention only and emphatically includes the female). Part II guides the writer toward certain questions and life experiences which his children and grandchildren will want to know about. One chapter is devoted to questions which can be asked of those interested in having their oral history recorded.

Some readers may wish to read the oral history section first, for some of the questions may provoke them to recollect stories and incidents from their past. For the reader interested primarily in recording the life of another—a mother, father, husband, etc.—the oral history type of narrative which results from these questions may be of great interest. It is more objective, less filled with subjective feelings, than the type of writing we have developed in our classes, but it is an honest accounting of the experiences of those whose lives are being described.

Some may wish to read this book through from beginning to end before starting to write, step by step. In that case, the reader may wish to jot down notes as ideas and incidents and people from the past come to mind.

The closing chapter suggests ways of putting one's memoirs together in a way that is pleasing to writer and to reader.

Part III is composed of selections from our life-story writing classes which demonstrate the various techniques we have developed and discussed. These techniques allow the reader a much more intimate sense of the writer's thoughts, feelings, and experiences than is normally the case in journal writing, oral history, and life narrative writing. The selections give a real taste of what we mean by "writing from within"— finding and capturing on paper the way life unfolded in vivid, emotional, intimate detail experienced from the point of view of the writer's age when the events occurred. Future editions of this text, which will be updated regularly, will contain new selections.

The reader and user of this self-help text is encouraged to go at the work in a leisurely manner. There is no need to rush through. It may take weeks or even months to move from one chapter to the next. That is to be expected. How many stories you do in each chapter is very much up to you. By the time you get to the chapter "Kids, Kids, Kids—and Parents Too" you may well have been working on your life's stories for six months to a year or longer.

In the first few weeks and months you will be spending a great deal of time rewriting, time that you might prefer to spend on the next recollection. To get the intimacy and depth of feeling and observation which is possible using the techniques described in the book, allow yourself the extra time and effort. Reread the book several times. In doing this, you will gradually make the techniques you have read and thought about a part of you. Using them will begin to feel comfortable. You will be happy with the results.

The stories which flow from these techniques will generally be arranged in chronological order; however, you, the writer need feel no compulsion to write them in that order. The stories need to be written as the inner urge dictates. I do suggest to my students that they write six to eight early memories, learning to write from the child's point of view (if possible) before they begin to skip around and write about different phases of their lives.

Part One

Acquiring
The
Techniques

CHAPTER ONE

OVERCOMING FEAR

To TELL ONE'S LIFE STORIES, TO LEAVE A memoir of the sad/happy, exciting/boring, fascinating/fearful experiences of one's long life seems like a wonderful idea. But how many wonderful ideas have we had in our lives which never became anything more than ideas? Quite a few? Yes, I suppose so. What stopped them from becoming reality? Probably lack of motivation or fear...or both.

If the idea of writing your own life story strikes a chord within you, sets off a bell, causes you to salivate (or fills you with unspeakable dread) then you are ready to write your story. What is holding you back is not lack of motivation. It is fear. Stark, naked fear.

Fear of what? Fear of being unable to write well and being criticized by friends and relatives; fear of being unable to finish, of getting off the track; fear that comes from believing you can't do it.

So there is a barrier. Let us take a closer look at it. Recent research into the way the brain operates suggests that there are two sides to the brain—left and right. Much of our fear of writing comes from the way these two sides do or don't work together.

The right brain apparently allows us to do creative things—make connections, create ideas, imagine situations of all kinds, see pictures of events. The left side analyzes things, puts them into categories, recalls words, and performs its learning functions in a step-by-step manner.

For our purposes what's important to know is that the analytic left brain has a little attic up on top which houses the "critic." He—or she—is the person in us who says, "Watch out! You can't do that! You'll fail, so don't even try. You know you're no good at that!"

And perhaps you would be right if you said that the critic sounds a lot like dear old mom or dad: "If I've told you once, I've told you a thousand times, you may not do (such and such) until you have carried out the garbage"—or cleaned out your room, done the dishes, gotten good grades, etc. Sound familiar? I'm sure it does. Believe me, I know. I, too, am a parent.

Well, parents are great. But they do tend to be critical. They are our guides in the world, but too often they do more than guide us. They tell us not to do certain things and we become afraid to do them.

The critic becomes a problem for us when we want to create something—a story or a painting—out of nothing because the right brain, in which our imagination stirs every now and then, is very tender, very sensitive to criticism. So if our left-side tough-minded parent-critic brain says, "Forget it! You can't do it," our right-side tender-minded imagination says, "Fine! OK! I'm going back to sleep. Talk to me again in a few weeks."

And so our deep desire to write our life story gets buried once again.

How do we counteract the critic? We calm him. We stroke him. When he comes out, we become aware of his presence but we do not fight him. We can enjoy his antics, be amused by his swordplay as he cuts away at our confidence, but we must keep out of range of that slashing saber. And we must avoid a confrontational stance with the critic: "What do you mean I can't do it! I can so!!" To the critic, that is merely a call to arms. On the other hand, a flexible stance—something like "You'll be surprised what I can do," or "I've been doing pretty well so I think I'll keep on creating, even if it seems kind of hard,"—will deflect the critic's thrusts and keep our creative juices flowing. So enjoy the critic, be amused by him, but don't try to duel with him. He is actually valuable at a later stage when he is calmer and able to look at your work objectively and can suggest ways and means of changing and editing it.

We human beings have an almost infinite variety of ways to censor ourselves. Fear not only keeps us from writing, it inhibits our letting the world see our work when it is done. We tend to be very hard on ourselves as writers. In fact, some very good work may be lost because of our pessimism.

The following is an example of a fine story which the writer had tossed in the garbage. The writer revealed what he had done almost by accident, and the class responded by insisting that he resurrect the story and bring it in. Here it is, complete with stains from coffee grounds and fried eggs.

My Friend Jake
by David Yavitts

From a small town in eastern Russia, our family arrived in the midwest of the United States, in St. Paul, Minnesota, a short distance from the banks of the Mississippi River.

Our house was on two and a half acres, partly in a hollow. The front of the house, that is, the parlor,

living room and dining room, were on street level.
The kitchen and bedroom were on the hollow portion, held up by posts.

It was there that life for me began in this country.
In the next couple of years, we had acquired a cow,
horse, chickens and ducks. My responsibility was
the ducks, keeping their quarters clean and feeding
them.

I became very fond of them, gave them names
and learned to recognize them by color and size. My
favorite duck I called Jake, because we got that particular duck from our neighbor Jake's farm.

As I spoke the English language poorly, I did not
have any friends, and I adopted Jake as my friend
and confidant. He listened to me and would cock his
head and did not move until I was through speaking. He would always wait for a while.

Jake grew faster than the other ducks and his
feathers, especially around his neck, were a ring of
black. The rest was white.

That winter the ducks became full grown and
plump. In the spring, I was assisting my mother in
cleaning the stove pipes. They were full of soot and
as I removed the soot much of the black powder
made my face and hands black.

It was time to feed the ducks and I couldn't find
Jake, my duck. I looked everywhere and called him.
There wasn't any response. I finally went into the
house; my mother was at the stove baking what she
said was a chicken. I explained to her that Jake, my
duck, was lost and that I couldn't find him. My
mother told me, if the duck was lost she would get
me another one—not to worry!

At this point, my older sister came in the kitchen
and said, "Is the duck done yet?"

The sky fell down and I shouted, "That's Jake!"
They could not pacify me. I cried and told them they

were mean and bad to kill Jake and I ran out of the house, saying I didn't want to live there any more. I said I was going to my uncle's house across the bridge, over the river.

They didn't believe it, but I started my journey.

I knew where the bridge was; I could see it from my home and headed in that direction. Here was a dirty-faced kid about three and a half who cried as he walked toward the bridge. In my mind, I knew my soft-hearted uncle would solve my problems.

Well, I didn't get very far on the bridge when I was stopped by a policeman who asked, "Where are you going, young man?"

He repeated that question many times. I did not understand too well. I spoke Yiddish and that soft-hearted Irish policeman spoke English with a brogue. He took me to the police station. There, an officer who understood me, got my story, figured out where I lived, left me at the station and eventually called my mother. She got my older sister out of the classroom at school and sent her to the station. My sister thought she would have to bail me out. There I was, my sister said, sitting on a table with an ice cream cone in my hand and crying. The tears ran down my face, washing the black soot off in white streaks. The ice cream washed my lips. I was a sight! My mother said, "Come home, dinner is waiting."

I said, "Mother, I don't eat duck!"

◊ ◊ ◊

Having finished the story, we can see it is complete and effective. The detail and observations are sharp; the dialogue is appropriate. It has a beginning, a middle, and an end; it is personal and deeply felt. Yet, despite its obvious excellence, the writer had dumped it in the trash. Imagine what would have happened, not only to the story, but also to the man's future as a writer, had the class not insisted that he retrieve it.

Once we understand how our left-brain critic works, we can begin to work on our memoirs knowing we can defuse our fears by identifying the pressure of the critic when he appears. Are you feeling more confident? Good. Now you are ready to begin working on your first memoir.

Chapter Two

Finding Your Earliest Memories

L
ET'S BEGIN WRITING" — THESE ARE WORDS
calculated to strike fear into the heartiest of souls,
particularly those who may not have touched pen to
paper in forty years or more. Calm yourself. The writing
process need not be traumatic. In fact, it can be fun.
Thinking about writing (or, more properly, worrying
about it) can be traumatic. So let's not think about it
right now. Let's do it.

"All right," you say, "suppose I have calmed my
fears. What do I write about? My life is dull, dull, dull."
The answer is that no life is dull; only the way it is
remembered and recorded is dull. We must find the
ways and means of getting to the interesting events and
people in our lives in a manner that is comfortable for
us, and real.

There are essentially three phases to writing a

memoir in an interesting, authentic way: composing it, reviewing it, and rewriting it. By following the specific steps which are part of each phase, you can be assured that your work will be readable and enjoyable.

Some of you may want to start by writing the life stories of your parents and grandparents. "They came first, so shouldn't I write what I know about them first?" you ask. The answer is: probably not. It is important to keep the family past distinct from your personal life story. Likewise, the quality of your writing about others will improve if you wait until you have developed your life-story writing skills.

So, the answer to your question, "What do I write about?" is, Write your earliest memory first. Your earliest memory is a good place to begin because it is something you see in your mind's eye, but it is not too complex to describe. It will probably be a fragment of something, a piece of a picture. That is just fine. It does not have to be a story. Even a few lines will do just fine. It's like doing "Twinkle, Twinkle, Little Star" when you were first learning to play the piano.

And you may be surprised at how interesting that little fragment really is. One of my students had been told all her life that she had hit her sister over the head with her baby bottle when she was still in the crib. What a traumatic memory to live with! But when she went way back to the actual incident, she recalled hitting the bottle on the side of the crib, and the bottle breaking and then hitting her sister. Suddenly, she was relieved of a guilt that had haunted her all her life, and the relief was wonderful!

Earliest memories are often dramatic—a birth or death in the family, leaving or arriving at someplace special, a medical emergency. Sometimes, though, they can be as simple as remembering a shiny thing that hung over your crib. No matter how simple, write down what you see in your mind. Just that. Nothing more.

COMPOSING

Composing is the first phase of writing your memoir, and involves the following:

Choose a comfortable place and time

Find a quiet, comfortable place in which you can work undisturbed (although European writers often prefer outdoor cafés where the noise seems to be strangely comforting); something relaxing in which to sit—a bed or a chair; a place where the light is adequate and not distracting. It is equally important to find the right time to write— usually sometime between eight in the evening and noon the next day. Our right-brain creativity is most at work during these times, whereas during the afternoon our left-brain, analytical energies are highest. So, if you don't feel like writing in the afternoon, don't force it.

Select a few familiar objects

Surround yourself with familiar objects which will remind you of your earliest experiences in life—photos, mementos, clothing, and other memories of your past.

Relax

Let us assume that having accomplished steps one and two, you are now trying to think. Perhaps you find yourself getting a little sleepy. You resist the urge, battling it for ten to fifteen minutes until finally you lose the battle and fall asleep. You awaken some time later feeling depressed; you have let yourself down. But you really have not. The next time this urge to sleep strikes you, give in to it. It's okay. It is your brain's way of switching from the everyday, problem-solving, left-brain mode to the creative, right-brain mode. "Go with the flow," as my teenage sons would say.

Return to the past

Use your daydream or reverie to channel your thoughts back toward the deep past. Now that you are comfortable and relaxed, and perhaps semi-sleepy, allow your mind to float back in time, way back to your first memory. It really doesn't matter whether you were three months old or three years old when it happened. It doesn't matter if it is not a story. It may be just a fragment of a picture. That is fine, as long as you *see* something. WRITE IT DOWN. NOW.

Write from a child's point of view

Write down what you have just seen in your mind's eye from the point of view of the baby or child you once were. If you were in a crib, the reader would expect to see a bit of the crib sticking up at the foot of the bed where momma and poppa might be staring down at you. Create a strong and vivid picture of what you see: the place where the event is occurring, the sounds and smells around you and the atmosphere of the scene. It is important to record all of these details. Once you have started to write do not stop until you have finished. Seeing the world through the eyes of a child, when the world was new and fresh, makes fascinating reading.

Now that you know what to do, it is time to do it. Are you ready to begin? Good. You are in that favorite, comfortable place, yes? There are no distractions. It is quiet outside and in. There are important objects around you, and you may even be a bit sleepy. Let your mind drift back, way back. You are very relaxed and your mind is going way back into the past...

REVIEWING

Having found your earliest memory and having written a first draft of it, you have completed the initial writing phase. The next phase is to review what you have done to see how your work comes across to a listener or reader. Like composing, the reviewing phase has several steps to be followed.

Resist the urge to make changes

The urge to make big changes and to be critical is always strong at this point. ("It *can't* be any good—I better change it.") Resist that temptation. Read over the story and make only a few corrections such as cleaning up grammar and usage. What you need most at this point is some feedback about the quality and effectiveness of what you have written.

Get feedback

Now you need to get some responses from friends and relatives about what you have written. It's rather scary to ask for reactions, but it will turn out okay. My own preference is to have a friend review it. A relative may be either too critical or too patronizing, and neither of these attitudes is helpful for a beginning writer. So find a friend and read it aloud to him or her. (See the Appendix "Developing Supportive Feedback" on page 228 for assistance on how to do this.)

Form a group

Working with a group of friends or acquaintances who are also interested in writing their life stories is very desirable, for several reasons. Reading memoirs aloud to a group will tell you whether your stories are coming across well or not. It is also fun to share remembrances of the past with friends, and often someone else's stories will remind you about similar experiences of your own. Another reason is that sharing stories with friends who are also interested in writing is less intimidating—everyone knows that his or her writing will be reviewed.

Write visually, for impact

Ask those who listen to your stories two things: Are the stories visual (can they see them clearly in their minds)? and, Do they have an emotional impact (what do the listeners feel as they listen to them)? Usually, if the story has an impact the listeners will tell you it reminded them of a similar time in their own lives. This is a very good sign.

Listen

Very often, you, the writer, will respond to comments, both positive and negative, by mentioning things, incidents, colors, materials, observations, jokes, reflections which you consciously or unconsciously decided to leave out. This is almost always vital information which needs to be in the story. So listen to yourself in class or with your friends, and flesh out the story with this information.

Achieve a "childlike" tone

Become aware of your story as a moment in time seen and experienced by a child. The story needs to be one which has simple vocabulary, reasonably short sentences, and is, above all, visual. Everything in it needs to be clear. If there is a tree between you and the sidewalk that has a fascinating caterpillar on one of its leaves, tell us about it. Be aware that you, the writer, must make us see that tree.

You now know the six steps to follow to review and evaluate your memoir properly. As an example of an earliest memory here is a short piece by Gina Wilcox.

CATERPILLAR
by Gina Wilcox

It was springtime, so I was about a year and three months old. We sat on the cement steps in front of our flat at 5959 Justine Street, Chicago. Mama plopped me down on the sidewalk and turned to gossip with shiny Aunt Rose. I could walk fast and slow, and do falling down and getting up all by myself. The smell of tar was very strong. The leaves of the tree had a lesser smell. They were oval shaped, coming to a point at the bottom with little stickers all around the edge. They seemed to have a life of their own. Each leaf came down in some other way of falling to me. Then that crawling thing began playing with me. A concertina shaped creature with fuzzy black hair and some yellow down around lots of little pointy feet. This piece of real live something bumped itself up to the middle, looked around, and proceeded. Bump up, look around, proceed; bump up, look around, proceed. Slowly and deliberately. It was like grandpa who sometimes had to walk with a slow hunch. When he did it just right, you could hear by his grunts that it wasn't hurting him. That was like this small moving creature. I didn't know what "caterpillar" was, so I did the only sensible thing I knew. I picked it up and put it in my mouth, or tried to. It wiggled out of my clutches. I followed, watching more carefully. When I felt the timing was right, I grabbed with my entire fist and squeezed. Some of the hairs came through between my fingers. It tickled. I dropped it. Off again! Gone into the cinders around the strong smelling tree. Mama called: "*Sto je ovo? Hodi ti simo.*" (What's going on? Come this minute!) I explained to her that I had discovered delicious moving things to play with and how happy I was.

◇ ◇ ◇

Notice how Gina allows us to experience all the sights, smells, tastes, and textures of things which are new and wonderful to a child, sensations which we as adults just take for granted.

REWRITING

We are now at the final phase of putting together your first memoir: rewriting. The first phase, composing, involved freeing you up to get your story down on paper without stopping, that is, without letting the critic grab hold of you and drag you back to redo that first paragraph, as so often happens. The second phase, reviewing, involved helping you to get some objective feedback about your work by having a friend or group listen and respond to it. In the final phase, rewriting, you will learn how to make your story more vivid and substantially clearer to the reader while deepening its impact.

Later on we will explore rewriting more thoroughly, but this first memoir needs only a bit of tinkering to make it work. It is, after all, just a moment from your childhood, probably not even a complete story. Like a pianist learning to play the scales, a note at a time, your present task is only to make this moment dramatic and believable.

When rewriting this first memoir, then, keep three rules before you:

1. Write visually

Be sure the story is made visible, with clear, vivid details.

2. Create emotional impact

Be aware of what your feelings were. Do you remember them? If you do, add in reactions like, "I felt scared," "I felt happy," etc.

3. Write from a child's point of view

This is perhaps the most important consideration

for this early story: Be sure your memoir sounds as if it were experienced by a child.

You are probably asking, "How in the world can I write as a child would when I'm not a child? Shouldn't I just write as an adult looking back?"

The answer is: "No." You may not be able to write exactly as a child would, but you can avoid certain writing patterns which mark the passages as those of an adult. You are, after all, trying to recapture the world as seen through a child's eyes, not an adult's eyes. Avoid using vocabulary, diction, and phrasing that a child could not possibly use. For example, consider the following passage:

> There were times, I suppose, when it seemed as if one would never be permitted to mature at a pace which was reasonable for my age. No, I was forced, albeit in a kindly fashion, to repeat *ad nauseam* the chores and duties attendant upon childhood: taking out the garbage, playing sports, minding my manners and obeying the strictures of my parents.

No one reading this passage would suppose for a moment that a child had written it. Why? Because children don't talk or write that way. Let us look at specific parts of this passage to see what is unchildlike about it.

Vocabulary and phrasing: "permitted to mature," "reasonable for my age," "*ad nauseam*," "attendant upon" are all phrases no child, other than one attending college at a remarkably early age, would ever use.

Qualifications: Statements which are qualified or modified are virtually never used by children. "I suppose" is a good example of a qualification, as is "albeit in a nice way."

The objective voice: "One" is the objective voice and is virtually never used by children.

Lists: Cataloging chores, etc., in an orderly manner is an adult way of organizing. Children may do it, but they are less orderly and logical.

Now, let us look at the passage after rewriting it in a way which may not be childlike but at least is not obviously adult.

> From the time I was six or seven until I was eleven, my dad insisted that I take out the garbage every Thursday. What a chore that was! It seemed as if he'd never give me any real responsibility, just chores. But I remember one time when he...

Here you have a voice which could be adult or child. The passage is simple, straightforward and visual. The narrator's voice and point of view do not intrude on the action or the progress of the story. So that the reader can see the differences between a childhood story and a rewrite told exclusively from a child's point of view, the first and second drafts of a story by Jade are given below.

WILLEM (1)
by Jade

I have no recollection of the first years of my life. Looking way back into my early childhood, I come up with this little picture, a picture that has surfaced every once in a while whenever I am thinking of the old days.

I must have been three or four. There was a big sprawling backyard. A tall hedge concealed the main house, some distance away. The house was quiet; my mother must be resting. It was siesta time, the time after lunch when the shimmering tropical heat made people drowsy. It was also Sunday, the drone of my father's machines was not there. My father must also be resting. My father had a house-industry at that time. He bought up spices such as pepper, nutmeg, cloves, cinnamon, etc. from the farmers overseas on the other island, then he ground and bottled them in a special building on the grounds. To assist him he asked Willem to come over from his hometown on a far island to work as his foreman. Willem also lived with us in an outhouse.

I liked Willem, because he always spent time with us, whenever there was a chance. That afternoon was no exception. He showed my brother and me some magic tricks and then he said, "Kids, I am going to show you how strong I am!" He asked Joni, another workman, to go fetch the bicycle. Then he lay down on the grass and Joni was told to drive over his chest. I was greatly impressed when Willem stood up unhurt. Then he said, "And now the van will drive over me." Again he lay down on the thick grass and supposedly the car drove over him. I was in awe that nothing happened to Willem. This was where I got befuddled. I am sure I had not told my mother then and there, because she would have taken some action regarding Willem's way of entertaining us and she would have remembered the incident. As it was, when years later I talked about it, mother said, "Nonsense, he must have tricked you." But I still wonder, did it really happen or was it just my imagination?

◊ ◊ ◊

After hearing the story, members of the class suggested that she simplify the vocabulary, and tell the story exclusively from the child's point of view, letting go of the inclination to set the stage which takes the reader out of the child's experience. We also suggested she write the story in the *present* tense. Here is the result.

WILLEM (2)
by Jade

I am sitting in the grass. The grass is cool and green and very thick and soft; I sink in it. I like to sit there. The sun is very bright, but the hedge behind me makes a shade.

My brother is there, too. He is bigger than I. Papa and Mama are not there. I know they are in the house a little far away behind the hedge. But Willem is there. He is very big, almost as big as Papa. I like him. He always has something nice for me and my brother.

What will he do today? He is lying in the grass. There is also Joni. I do not know him too well, but he does not matter. Willem is there!

Willem is saying: "*Anak mau lihat Willem digiling sepeda?*" ("Kids, want to see the bike run over me?") Joni already goes to fetch the bicycle. There he comes—straight at Willem lying in the grass. Then the bicycle is already on the other side of Willem and Willem is standing up and laughing. He laughs at us kids. And then, with a laugh in his eye, he tells us, Papa's big truck will now run over his chest. Again he lies down in the thick grass—the car comes and it is over him—only his head sticks out—he is laughing at us. I hide my head. I am afraid and I grab my brother's hand. But I still look. Willem is already up again. Willem can do anything!!!

Years later when I talked about it, mother said, "Nonsense, he must have tricked you." But I still wonder, did it really happen?

◊ ◊ ◊

Notice that while we lose some information we gain a great deal in dramatic impact, particularly when we write in the present tense. By writing from the child's point of view and revealing only what the child can see right in front of her eyes, we are brought very close to the event.

If, at the *end* of this memory or subsequent early memories, you would like to add some background information and/or some of your present adult feelings about what happened back then, do so. But keep the adult reflection on the event clear and distinct from the child's point of view. Jade's last line, "Years later when I talked about it, mother said...but I still wonder..." is a good example of including an adult reflection while keeping it distinct from the child's experience.

In successive stories we will continue to write from the child's point of view, although as we get older we naturally know more of past and present and can set the stage more fully. Please see Roz Belcher's story, "Goin' South" (page 148) as an example of a powerful memory seen from a child's point of view.

Note: During your first rewrite you may find that writing from the child's point of view is difficult. If this happens, go on to the next assignment and come back to writing or rewriting from the child's point of view at a later time.

◊ ◊ ◊

Now that you have finished writing your earliest memory, you have done what every writer does: Composed, reviewed, and rewritten. These are the same three steps you will follow with every story you write. As you write your earliest memories, you will find that even earlier incidents and experiences will return. The actual process of putting pen to paper seems to call up memories. Write these as soon as they become vivid and significant. Many life experiences block feelings, and writing unblocks these feelings and allows you to move ahead, free and unencumbered.

CHAPTER THREE

FINDING YOUR
EARLIEST
POWERFUL
MEMORY

IT MAY BE HARD TO BELIEVE, BUT YOU ARE NOW a writer. you have written a memoir, received some response, rewritten it and read it to your friends or relatives. In all probability they liked it. Of course, "one memoir does not a writer make," but be good to yourself. Accept the praise. And congratulations! Now you are ready to go on to the next memory or series of memories.

This one may be a little more difficult. You've done a few scales and a simple tune; now we'll try you out on something harder. At the same time we will look for more places to improve your work during the reviewing phase and do more tinkering in the rewriting phase.

This time you are going to go back into the past in search of the earliest *powerful* memory you can find, a memory that stands out more than any other early memory. It may be an escape from a threatening situation when you were a child; it may be the death of a dear friend or relative; it may be a time in your life when you left or came to live at a special place; or it may be meeting a special person for the first time. Whatever the memory, now is the time to write about it.

COMPOSING

Begin composing by following the same five steps which were outlined in Chapter Two, directing your mind back toward your earliest possible powerful memory, one that truly stands out in high relief in your mind.

This early *powerful* memory should not be confused with your earliest memory, which may simply be a tiny fragment of recollection, like some archaeological relic from a prehistoric time. No, we are looking for an early memory that has power, a memory that is very strong.

So, get ready to return now to your storehouse of childhood experiences. Are you sitting in that easy chair? Is the music on low? Is the fire about right? Are you ready to return to the time tunnel? All right then, back you go...to another distant moment in time. Keep those details in view; search out lost ones as well. Strip away the wrappings around the memory until you can see it clearly.

◊ ◊ ◊

When you feel that you are again "conscious," write down everything you saw and experienced, at once. Don't stop, even if the pieces are disconnected. Don't stop, even if the memory makes you want to cry. If that happens, okay. But keep writing. Now, how does the story read? Is it one story or fragments? Are the details sharper than in your first memoir? Are the feelings stronger? If you have written a series of fragments, would you like to fill in the gaps? If not, okay; go ahead and take this memoir to your group. Read it aloud and listen carefully to each response.

REVIEWING

During this second phase we will learn more about what to look for when evaluating our own writing, and how to listen and offer critiques in a helpful manner when other people read their stories to us.

Let us begin with a checklist of the first steps in reviewing:

— resist the urge to change, to be too critical

— get feedback, form a group to get responses from other people

— ask if the work is visual and emotion-producing

— listen to your own comments to see if something was left out

— express your stories as experiences seen from a child's point of view

Now let us go into some of these concerns a bit more thoroughly. Recalling the rewriting instructions of the previous chapter, we see that it is important to write visually and create emotional impact. Two ways in which we can enhance the visual clarity of the story is through the use of *detail* and by bringing the story closer to the reader with appropriate *dialogue.*

Detail

The first objective in writing good narrative stories is to make the events visible. The easiest way to do this is to bring the event into sharp focus by including little details which make the picture unique. Look at the following passage by Rose Rothenberg:

> Uncle Eli was a dapper man and extremely meticulous about his person. His shirts were always pure white, at least until they yellowed a bit with age. His dark serge suit was always well pressed and clean. It did not yellow with the passage of time, but took on a shine that competed with the gloss he maintained on his high-button shoes. In the summer months he sported spotless white buckskin oxfords—the same pair year after year. His straw hat was worn at a rakish angle and, rain or shine, he was never without an umbrella. (Taken from the story on page 177.)

The details in this passage—shirts "always pure white until they yellowed with age," the suit that "took on a shine," and the umbrella that was carried "rain or shine"—tell us a great deal about the man's character: his stubbornness, inflexibility and pride in the face of changing circumstances.

Now let us look at another passage rich with details which reveal a great deal. This is from Eugene Mallory's "Life on the Railroad." (See page 152.)

> The year was 1904. Not a good year for the overbuilt, midwestern railroads or the ever-distressed farmer either.
>
> The Missouri Pacific Red Ball freight was two hours out on a night run west. The nearly new Baldwin 4-8-2, burning clean Colorado coal, was really showing what it could do.
>
> Conductor William Sidel was riding the high seat in the cupola of the darkened caboose and pondering what he should do with his upside down life in general. First as a boomer brakeman, so called because he and many other bold young men had followed the railroad expansion of the late 1800s

wherever the new rails led. Always moving on to new runs, new towns.

Then a bit of luck, and a bit of the old blarney, and he had his own train on the Hampton, Algona and Western, riding the varnish, not a crummy caboose. Even if the varnish was only an old combination coach; half seats, half mail and baggage, and his little conductor cubbyhole. The coach had to be there to satisfy the franchise, and he had trundled it up and down the 90 miles of lightweight rail that was all the Hampton, Algona and Western ever amounted to. No matter that many grand names had been painted over or that the old coach was hung on the end of an untidy string of freight cars and seldom exceeded 20 miles per hour, it was varnish.

A perfect old man's job, while he was still young, had perhaps made him old in too few years. God forbid!

But why was he uneasy on this perfect prairie night? True, when he had totaled his manifests, the weight of this train had shocked him, and now, his certified reliable watch said they had covered 40 miles of track in the last hour. Things had changed while he had vegetated on the "branch"...

The phrase "riding the high seat in the cupola of the darkened caboose and pondering what he should do with his upside down life" gives us a vivid picture of a man perched up high, looking out on the moving train and looking inward on his life in the darkness. Another phrase, "no matter that many grand names had been painted over," gives us an equally vivid picture of time passing.

These phrases are good examples of the power of well-chosen details to convey information and feeling. As a writer, you will choose your own details as you remember them. What you will want to avoid is giving lots of details about objects when you are describing, say, a room or a place. Select details carefully, otherwise they can become repetitive and boring. The most interesting and useful details seem to be those which give a glimpse of *what* people do and *why* they do it.

Dialogue

Have you ever heard this comment from one of your classmates or friends: "It was a good story and the details were good, but I still didn't feel close to what was happening?" If so, there is another technique which will help you bring the reader or listener closer to the action: dialogue. Not a lot. Just a little, in fact. Begin by trying to remember what your characters actually said way back when. If you can't quite remember what they said, write down what they might have said. As you do that, something inside of you will say, "Yes, that's close," or "No, that doesn't feel right at all." That same voice will carry you closer to what actually was said provided you write, not just think, the words you are seeking. In general, try to keep your dialogue to a sentence or two each time a character speaks. Here is an example of good dialogue, well remembered.

JEFFERSON BARRACKS, MISSOURI
John Strong

We stepped outside for some fresh air. As luck would have it, the pigeon air corps was practicing dive bombing with Ford's new green sweater as the target.

"Why did those damn pigeons pick on me?" lamented Ford, as he tried to wipe the droppings from his sweater with his handkerchief.

"Because they knew we were headed for the Air

Corps and wanted to show us some expert bombing!" I joked.

"This isn't funny, John," protested Ford.

"Maybe they hate Irishmen and you're Irish and
wearing green," I laughed.

"But you're Irish and a bigger target. Why didn't
they pick on you?"asked Ford.

"Oh, can it, Ford," I yelled. "I'll give you the
money to get it cleaned. This is trivial compared to
the army life we've gotten into."

"Maybe Jefferson Barracks will be better," offered optimist Bill. But when we pulled into St.
Louis next morning, Ford was still talking about the
big stain on his sweater, the size of a pancake.

I went to a phone in the station, collecting my
thoughts for my official call to Jefferson Barracks
as the officer at Harrisburg had instructed.

"Sir, this is Recruit John Strong, with recruits
Bill Bee and Ford Smith. We are coming from Harrisburg, Pennsylvania. I have all the necessary
papers," I recited in a good strong voice, trying to
make a favorable impression.

On the other end of the line, I heard a child-like
voice squealing, "What son of a bitch stole my comic
book? It was a Dick Tracy one, too. Come on, cough
it up." Then he grumbled to me, "Say that again,"
which I did.

His next words really startled me. "What the hell
do you expect me to do about it?" I thought I had a
Captain's young son on the phone, so I remained
silent for a moment. "You got a tongue, ain't you.
Now tell me what you want me to do," the brat
ranted. "I have no papers on you at all."

"Maybe you can suggest how we can get to Jefferson Barracks," I offered, with a slight sneer in
my voice.

"No one told me you were coming. The only way

you can get here is in the mail truck. It's due at the station in about fifteen minutes, so get your asses to the entrance or you will have to walk the fifteen miles to get here. If you don't get here by midnight, you will be A.W.O.L." With that, the jerk slammed the phone down.

(Continued on page 187.)

◊ ◊ ◊

Notice that new characters are introduced quickly through dialogue: "I heard a child-like voice squealing, 'What son of a bitch stole my comic book.' " Soon we learn this is his new commanding officer—a quick, unexpected glimpse of a new character. This is good dialogue at work.

Tips on listening effectively and giving concise feedback

Listening constructively to the stories other writers are telling can help us develop objectivity about our own work. It also helps to develop a rapport with the other writers, who might welcome our feedback, and is a source of new ideas.

The first rule in "reviewing" others' work is: Proceed with caution. Our biggest problem as listeners is that we want to be right—and righteous. We want to be able to make the smartest comment, and we want to say nothing that will expose us to criticism.

If we say too much, we will sound critical and may discourage the writer with our negativity. If we say too little—"I liked it," "that was very nice,"—we may give him or her nothing to work with, or may give a false sense of effectiveness.

Begin by paying close attention to your feelings. Ask yourself, How do I feel after listening to this story? Does it touch my emotions? Does it make me happy or sad, carefree or thoughtful? Then tell the writer what your feelings are.

Is the story memorable? Could you see everything the writer was writing about? Were there plenty of vivid, fresh details throughout? Can you remember them? Let the writer know just how visual his or her story is.

If you are the writer, note carefully how you respond and what you say when class members comment on your story. Try not to defend yourself. Just explain, if you feel you need to, what was behind some of the creative decisions you made. Even more important, listen to yourself. What you say to your friends after you have read the story aloud will provide valuable information which you may have excluded in your first draft. Often a classmate will ask a provocative question, one which you, the writer, would like to have asked yourself in the first place. Writers frequently answer questions offhandedly, only to realize they have revealed important information or details that would flesh out the story. So, as a writer, listen to what you say during these question-and-answer periods.

Follow these suggestions and you will find your group discussions becoming more and more helpful as well as interesting.

REWRITING

You are now ready to begin rewriting your second story. You have a greater fund of techniques at your disposal and a more thorough grasp of what these techniques can do. You have the responses of your friends or classmates to help you. Likewise, you have a better grasp of how to look at your own work after writing that first draft.

We tend to think of rewriting as very taxing, perhaps boring, maybe even painful. But the results are almost always worth the effort. To have one's work go straight through to the mind and heart of the reader feels wonderful to a writer, as you are no doubt finding out. For those of you interested in seeing how a story can be expanded and enriched in the rewriting process take a look at "The Typhoon of Forty-Five," by Ed Boyle (see page 161). This thirteen-page epic began as a three-page story, and both versions are included for you to read.

At this point, review the steps we discussed in rewriting your first memoir—

1. write visually

2. include your feelings

3. write from a child's point of view if your stories are about childhood

—and add to them the concerns we have just mentioned in our review phase: details and dialogue. Do not try to rewrite on a step-by-step basis, however. Once you have given thought to these various areas of improvement, read your story over and make gut-level corrections where it feels right to do so.

Focus

That leaves one more concern, which may not have arisen in connection with writing your earliest memory. A powerful memory may in fact be a series of powerful memories, so you must develop a sense of when the episode begins and ends, and write only one episode at a time. This is called focus. Classically, in an Ibsen play for example, a play begins only after some important event has taken place—a death, a crime, etc. In your work you may start with a similar event, or just before the event starts. What is important is to get the reactions of the major characters throughout the episode, then know when the incident or event ends. Focus is also related to finding the spine, which we will discuss in greater detail in Chapter Five under "Form and

Structure."
    Now go ahead and rewrite.

◊ ◊ ◊

    Having done your rewriting, take it to your friends, relatives and classmates. I think you will be pleasantly surprised. And if you want to write several "powerful memories" before going on, do so.

CHAPTER FOUR

DESCRIBING
INTERESTING PEOPLE

UNLIKE THE LILLIPUTIANS IN *GULLIVER'S Travels*, into whose world a big person was suddenly cast, we are all born into a world of big people. Mothers and fathers, in particular, loom especially large in our lives and in our imagination. Sometimes they appear distorted. My father, for example, appeared to most people as a strong-minded, humorous, thin-skinned and occasionally imperious man. To me, as I was growing up, he appeared so powerful that, until well into my thirties, I had dreams in which he appeared as a pursuing monster and I was a frightened Lilliputian.

Family members, many of whom have great power over us, must be dealt with in our memories honestly, clear-sightedly and fearlessly. Since our view of them will change as we grow older, it is both appropriate and necessary to see them as they were experienced by other members of the family and by ourselves at different times of our lives.

COMPOSING

Let's consider what makes a character in a book, a play or a movie "interesting," and see how it applies to our parents and the rest of the family. We might begin with the following definition: Someone who wants something badly (*what* he wants is usually very clear) and takes an interesting, unusual or difficult route to get that goal (*how* he is going to get it is also clear) is interesting. To the degree that the goal is dangerous and the means employed involve risk, the person might move up the scale from interesting to heroic.

Character qualities

How a person goes about getting what he or she wants reveals certain character qualities. Charm, determination, humor, honesty, self-assurance, dependability, opportunism, perfectionism are all qualities which get us what we want; they may also, tragically, defeat us in other ways.

At this point I would like you to read two stories. The first one is "Uncle Eli" by Rose Rothenberg (page 177), and the question is, can you tell what the central character, Uncle Eli, wants? The second story, "Escape to Freedom" by Rose Saposnek (page 182), is about a mother bringing her daughter out of Russia during the pogroms of the Russian Revolution of 1917. Determining what she wants is not difficult, but see if you can identify her character qualities. In both stories, try to figure out what incidents reveal how interesting and/or heroic these people are.

After you have had a chance to read about and discuss several kinds of interesting characters, take some time to write about one yourself.

Follow these five steps:

1. Think of a character you consider interesting.

2. Recall an incident, event or series of actions which were typical of this character.

3. Find a word for the memorable quality or qualities he or she possesses.

4. Ask yourself if the incident you recalled really brings out the quality you have identified. If it does, then go ahead and write about it; if not, then you may wish to select a different incident.

5. Remember that the most interesting characters have several strong qualities, sometimes contradictory ones.

In the process of remembering and then writing about important experiences that involve another strong character, two questions arise which we, as writers, should begin to consider. First, can we find a window through which the reader will see the events which we are portraying as we saw them: a window which will help the reader see exactly where and when the event began and ended, and where he or she is perched throughout the story? Second, can we find a way to write about what *we* were feeling as we were involved with or watching this person? Understanding the answers to these questions and weaving them into a narrative are tasks for the reviewing and rewriting phases of your assignment, so don't give them more thought just yet.

◊ ◊ ◊

Now lean back, let those images ripple up from the murky depths of time to the surface of the present. The waters are calmer now, the place and person clearer than before.

REVIEWING

In reviewing your latest memoir, keep in mind all of the things you have learned earlier, while adding new items to the "stew." In fact you might want to make a checklist of questions to ask yourself, like pilots who go through a list of proper procedures before take-off and landing. The checklist would be composed of a series of questions from earlier reviews plus new considerations, and might look like this:

1. Is my story visual?

2. Does it have emotional impact?

3. Is it told from a consistent point of view? A child's perhaps?

4. Do the details make the story clearer and more interesting?

5. Does the dialogue help tell the story and make the characters more interesting?

6. Have I kept to one, well-focused incident at a time?

7. Are the characters' "qualities" evident?

In reviewing the memoir, you will want to continue to add to your techniques and concerns, so we will now address two additional aspects of writing: setting the stage, and finding emotion in the facts.

Setting the stage

When a story begins, a number of questions arise in the reader or listener almost immediately: what is going to happen, who is doing what to whom, why is it happening, and where is it taking place. A good story will address all of these questions soon after the curtain goes up, and will answer most of them by the time the curtain descends. "Setting the stage" answers the question, "Where are we?" Another way to ask it would be: "From what position or angle are we viewing the action?"

Exactly where a writer or an artist positions us will have a powerful influence on the meaning of the story or incident we are viewing. This may be easier to understand with a painting, so let us look at two examples. The first is Leonardo DaVinci's "The Last Supper."

We are placed directly in front of Christ, able to see the effects on either side of him of his statement, "One of you shall betray me." We are neither below nor above the action, neither awed by nor superior to it. It is happening directly in front of us, in a clearly defined space in which a fifteenth century Tuscan valley unfolds behind the head of Christ. We know where we are, and from what position we are seeing the action. It is "real" to us. This is our perspective.

Another interesting example is Peter Breughel's "The Fall of Icarus." Here we are placed high on a hill overlooking a distant harbor early in the sixteenth century in a place that resembles Northern Europe.

We are placed near a peasant whose chores will take him down and to the left in the painting. Our eye is led to the distant vistas: to the new "round" world beyond. Because of our position near the peasant we would most likely ignore anything in the lower right portion of the painting such as the leg of Icarus, who has just fallen out of the sky. (You may recall that Icarus and Daedalus escaped from the labyrinth of King Minos by making wings of wax. Though advised by his father not to fly too close to the sun, Icarus disobeyed and plunged ignominiously into the sea when his wings melted.)

What is the meaning of this painting? Perhaps something like, "We are all so preoccupied with our daily tasks, we hardly see the truly important events in life taking place. We are distracted by the boring neces-

sities of life (the peasant's tasks) and the world's concerns (opening up the world and viewing it, not as flat but as round)."

The settings of these paintings and the perspectives from which we view the action have a great deal of influence on their message and impact on us, and it is similar with stories. For examples of how a story can be framed or introduced, look at the following stories in Part III: Eugene Mallory's "Life on the Railroad" (page 152) and Rose Saposnek's "Escape to Freedom" (page 182).

In each case you, the reader, are quickly transported to another time and place. You can see quite vividly the setting and surroundings in which the story happens. This is the key: to be able to see the surroundings as clearly as if they had been photographed. In terms of cinematic technique you might say that first comes the establishing shot, a wide-angle shot encompassing a whole city or village; next, a medium shot bringing us closer to the particular dwellings or places we are going to inhabit for the next few minutes or so; finally, a closer shot of the characters important to this narrative.

On the other hand, many modern films begin with a tight shot, then widen to include everything important. If you are writing stories of your life when you were younger than ten years old, that is, writing from a child's point of view, establishing shots might actually be unbelievable at the beginning of a story. The child's world is a very tiny and narrow though fascinating one. So an establishing shot—a more comprehensive, adult view—might actually come at the *end* of the scene or story. After the story ends you may also wish to tell the reader how the event described has affected you over the ensuing years.

Now let's look at another problem in "setting the stage." Suppose you had been told a story about a hurricane by your father or grandfather. And suppose that you would like to tell the story accurately, in considerable detail. In the interests of accuracy you could choose to leave out details that your grandfather or father could only guess at (making the story less interesting). Or you could include the details as if you had seen them (which is not true). Fortunately, you have another alternative, which is to describe the action as vividly as possible, then own up to the fact that the events were told to you: "This is the way my father described it, as well as I can remember." And in the places where even he didn't see it, you can simply say, "Pa surmised that..."

Remember when setting the stage that describing a setting is not necessarily a matter of inspiration. One need not go into a creative trance in order to create a solidly visual picture. In fact, the beginning of the story can be lightly sketched in at first, and the details of time and place filled in later, when the story is about to be completed. Do not get bogged down in details of time and place when you are first setting down your narrative.

Finding emotion in the facts

By now you've had a chance to listen to narratives from the other members of your group. Have you noticed that some of the stories or incidents really stir up emotions in you while others, though they may be descriptive and have good dialogue, just don't do anything? Perhaps your narrative is one of these. You may be defending yourself, saying, "That's how I remember things," but still, something is missing. Well, there are ways of getting more feeling into your writing, ways which will cause readers or members of your group to remember your story and say, "Now that really stirred me up."

First, however, let us back up for a moment. We

have talked about the difference between the right and left brains. Are you aware that there are also different "eyes" with which to see? Yes, that's what you read, different eyes.

Oh, I know we have two eyes which are plainly visible to everyone, eyes on either side of our nose, eyes which look out on the world and tell us how it is. Some anthropologists and paleophysiologists, however, believe there is evidence of an ancient "third" eye located in the middle of the forehead: the eye of the Cyclops. This third eye may or may not actually exist, but what is important is that this third eye is the eye of self-awareness, the eye of the inner world. In particular, it is the eye of knowing how we *feel* as we watch, observe and participate in the experiences of the outside world. Using our third eye, we can record our feelings and reactions to events as they go by.

This would be a good time to read a short passage which reveals what the writer is feeling as well as seeing in her mind's eye.

I see Kate as she was then in the bloom of her youth, yet so oddly old beyond her years. Her lustrous, red, wavy hair was worn shoulder length, parted on the side, brushed away from her rather plain face and held in place with a barrette. Stylish tortoiseshell glasses failed to hide the pain reflected in her pale brown eyes. A sprinkling of freckles spotted her forehead and extended into the areas just under the eyes.

Kate was a pleasant, soft-spoken, agreeable girl, but often seemed distant, as if only a part of her were involved with the present. Quite often, too, when her features relaxed in a lovely, wide-mouthed smile, her eyes remained sad, remote.

The sadness I perceived in her spoke to a certain melancholy of my own spirit that surfaced now and then, and I was drawn to her. But our friendship was slow to mature.

In these paragraphs from Rose Rothenberg's "A Lost Soul" (page 198), we can find numerous phrases which evoke emotions about the person being described: "bloom of her youth...oddly old...glasses failed to hide the pain reflected in her pale brown eyes," and finally, "her features relaxed in a lovely, wide-mouthed smile, [but] her eyes remained sad, remote." We also get a picture of the writer's feelings: "The sadness I perceived in her spoke to a certain melancholy of my own spirit that surfaced now and then, and I was drawn to her."

So we can see that with this third eye, the eye of awareness, we not only detect a certain sadness in her friend, we also notice how our own sadness is touched by hers. The emotion in the object of the description, Kate, is echoed by the emotion in the writer, Rose Rothenberg, and this is clearly communicated to us. In this way we find emotion in the facts.

REWRITING

Rewriting now becomes easier because you know what has to be done and you have a variety of techniques with which to approach the task. At this point, look over your checklist, begin to visualize any changes you may wish to make, then make them.

Setting the stage is related to writing from a child's point of view in this way: As a young child I see the world through a very tiny and narrow window. I know little of what others are doing; I know nothing of past and future. It is a narrow and very particular stage setting. As I mature, the window through which I see the world widens; I know more of past and present, of life beyond myself, therefore I can set the stage more fully.

As a writer, I ask my reader to suspend his or her

normal disbelief and believe what I have written. From a child, the reader can only believe the world as seen through the tiny window of a small child's awareness, but from a more mature youngster or an adult the reader can accept a much more fully set stage.

Chapter Five

Finding
And Describing
A Place Memory

H AVING WRITTEN YOUR FIRST MEMORY AND your first powerful memory, and perhaps several of those, as well as one or two memories of interesting people, you are now ready to go on to the next important step: writing a memory of a place where vital, unforgettable things happened. It could be a place from childhood or from a later time. Try, however, to find these memories in your childhood, if you can.

Up to this point we have described incidents and characters from our past. But some of you are itching to describe a bigger picture of who you are and where you have come from. You can start by describing a place which generated experiences affecting you or members of your family.

So that you can see how this sort of thing is done, I have included a selection by Hal Brand, set in the apartment house in which he was raised as a child. The great virtue of this kind of place memory is that it can set the stage for many wonderful incidents, and for the comings and goings of many delightful and whimsical characters who can reappear later in the narrative.

Notice how this writer has included a brief, physical description of each main character and highlighted some outstanding quality, either positive or negative, a quality which we easily remember.

SQUARE PEG
by Hal Brand

New York, New York, a wonderful town, was my birthplace.

We lived in a rather expensive apartment house located on 147th Street between Broadway and Amsterdam Avenue, in the area on Manhattan Island called Washington Heights. It was the year 1913, just before we entered the First World War.

On Broadway were the stores for shopping, and Amsterdam Avenue was where the lower priced walk-up apartments were located. They were occupied by Irish families and several other ethnic groups. The Irish boys were tough, and later on I had to learn to avoid some of them, as they disliked Jewish boys. They were always looking to promote a fight with the "mockies," as we were called. We called them "micks." In a way, they were envious of where and how we lived.

My father was a successful millinery manufacturer. He was strictly a businessman and did very little to participate in my period of growing up. His was the sales part of the business, as his brother took care of the production in the factory. He was away very often on selling trips.

Our apartment house was a six-story building,

with a fancy entrance and a large lobby with marble floors. In the rear of the lobby was an ornate elevator which had a fancy grillwork. There was a man on duty twenty-four hours a day to operate it. Should the elevator break down, on the left-hand side of it was a marble staircase, which went to the sixth floor. Our apartment on the fifth floor was large and spacious in the rear of the building. The windows faced the backyard and the rear of the building on the next street. Many times as I grew older, I saw interesting things happen in that building when the shades were up. That building was not as fancy as ours, as the tenants were not in our income bracket. However, my parents had several friends who lived there. One of the families was named Falk. Mr. Falk was a cellist in the New York Philharmonic. Many times in later years we visited them. At that time he entertained us by playing the cello. This was my first introduction to classical music, which is still one of my greatest pleasures.

Living on the fifth floor raised problems; there had to be some way that the ice could be delivered by the iceman. In those days everyone had an icebox. Also, bottles had to be delivered by the milkman. Therefore we had a dumbwaiter which could be loaded in the basement and pulled up to the fifth floor. Then the iceman with his tongs would come upstairs and put the large pieces in the box. There are always stories going around about icemen having relationships with the wives while the husbands were away at work. Knowing my mother's strict ethics, I know this never happened.

On the third floor of the building, in an extra-large apartment, lived my mother's family. It consisted of three bachelor uncles and two spinster aunts. In a fashion, they influenced my childhood as they were always interfering and advising my mother how I should be raised. They were of German descent and believed in a strict, disciplined upbringing. I never had much love for them, except my Aunt Annie, who was partially crippled. She was a sweet, lovable person. Maybe it was her deformity which made her different from the others. When I went to visit them, she would give me home-baked cake and cookies.

From the time I was born, we had a black nanny named Viola, who lived with us. She took care of me, giving me the best of care. She did the cooking and cleaning, which enabled my mother to follow her charitable pursuits. Since Viola was there, my parents were able to go visiting and to travel.

Three years after my birth, my sister Ruth was born. Viola now had two children to raise, and as usual did her very efficient job. I had no sibling rivalry toward my sister. To this day, there is still love between us. Even though our temperaments are considerably different, we are very close and accept each other with compromises.

The only grandparent that was still living at the time was my grandfather on my father's side. He lived alone in the Bronx and made occasional trips to visit us. He never came empty-handed, always bringing an apple for me. Why an apple I never knew. It must have stood for something to him. There was the old saying, "An apple a day keeps the doctor away." He was a quiet, kindly old man and I had great affection for him. When he passed away, I missed him and his apple. However, death did not have any meaning to a child. In due course of time he faded from my memory, and was merely part of my growing up picture.

The person for whom I developed the greatest affection was my mother's aunt, whose name was Lena. She had emigrated to the United States as a young girl. Her family settled on the lower East Side of New York. She enjoyed living there in what was called a railroad flat. It had a long hall with apartments on both sides of it. The location was Hester Street, in a walk-up building. Even though my father offered to move her to an apartment near us, she continually turned him down. That was where she had come as a young girl, and that was where she wanted to end her days. At the time I was born she must have been in her sixties, which was quite old for someone in the early 1900s. She was the sweetest, kindest person that I have ever known. Visiting us was one of her pleasures, and when she did, it was always for a few days. She was an excellent cook, and made the best German dishes. She was also a good baker and her cakes and cookies were terrific. I grew to love her, and when she passed away it was a blow. To this day I have a recollection of her as a short, slightly heavy woman with a smiling face. I can recall my parents taking me to visit her on Hester Street. The lower East Side had a character all its own. With the pushcarts and basement stores, it was very different from 147th Street, where we lived. Her apartment was filled with ceramic knick-knacks, and on the wall old pictures hung. This was her place and she fit it perfectly. It isn't very often in one's lifetime that an Aunt Lena comes along.

◊ ◊ ◊

In writing about a place of importance to you, remember it is *what happened* in this place and *to whom it happened* that will be of interest to the reader. Yes, the mood, atmosphere, and detail of the place are important, but it is the movement of things and people in and around this place that will make it memorable.

Now, let's prepare to write what you have experienced but without getting bogged down in details. Are you ready now to turn to the past, to tell the reader about incidents and people in and around that special place? You are in that comfortable, quiet space of yours. You are relaxed; your mind is directed back toward the deep past to a place where something interesting or special happened. Go ahead, begin writing...

REVIEWING

As we come to the reviewing phase of our work, we will add two other elements to our checklist:

1. a concern for form and structure in the story

2. improvising with the facts when memory fails

Form and structure: finding the spine

Form is a tricky thing to talk about with writers. It is one of those things that all writers and writing teachers love to discuss. Knowledge of form is what makes a writer an expert, just as being able to fill cavities is what makes a dentist an expert. Or at least that is what writers like to believe.

Essentially, form gives one's work some definable shape, so that the readers or listeners may know where they are going and can enjoy where they have been. A story about a duck needs to be about a duck. A story about an abortion needs to be about an abortion. A story about an uncle needs to be about an uncle. As a writer, this involves giving the reader or listener little clues about what to look for or listen for, a coherent thread or even a running gag. For example, in John Strong's "Jefferson Barracks" series you will notice that Ford's handkerchief eventually becomes a running gag. John mentioned it a few times, got a ton of laughs, and then began to plant it, rather artfully, at other places in the narrative. This is form.

Sometimes a mood or an atmosphere running through a story can also provide form. For example, in Gene Mallory's haunting stories of his Iowa past, the stories, almost like the trees and houses he describes, hang heavy with memory and emotion (see page 61). This, too, is form.

Each story has its own emotional logic, its own concerns, and the line of that logic is the spine. Anything else should be left aside. Other concerns, issues, people, need to be dealt with at a later time. Finding, then keeping to the spine is closely related to structure. Since the mind can hold just so many things in it at one time, we have to limit the mind's attention to those things that are related to the spine.

Let's suppose, for example, the beginning of our story is about taking a trip from Russia to the U.S.A., the middle is about finding a house to settle in so that Mom, who is sick, can feel better, and the end of the story is about Mom's death and how everyone felt.

From the ending, we get a clue about the spine and the structure. In fact, the middle—Mom's getting sick—is also a clue. The beginning needs to relate to the end, so the beginning of the story needs to be about Mom's health or well-being. The trip from Russia is clearly a separate story.

In the story you read earlier, "Square Peg," the spine of the story is the various people who live in and around the writer's apartment house, a spine which allows the writer to develop other stories around the lives of these people.

◊ ◊ ◊

These are the things you want to think about during your left-brain, rewriting phase. As you become more skilled you can start to think about the form of your story *before* you begin writing; for now, form is a concern of the rewriting phase of your work.

Improvising: Filling in the gaps where memory fails

As you continually dig up and confront your memories, you may begin to feel like something of an archaeologist. The brain is a magnificent and fascinating organ, fascinating because it often yields up what it wishes to give us, not what we think it ought to be giving us. Within its rich bank of memories you have undoubtedly discovered several fragments of recollections which seem to form a whole, but somehow you cannot complete it—the names, places and times that are the links between the fragments appear to be lost. As a result, you may feel stuck and unable to write or complete that memoir.

The experienced archaeologist not only knows where to dig for artifacts of the past, but, when they are in hand, he knows how to put them together in such a way that he can make educated guesses about ancient habits, customs and beliefs. The past becomes clearer.

So, what does one do if one simply doesn't have enough evidence to create the links to complete the story that is lurking inside one's brain? Frustrating, isn't it? To know that one's most interesting memory is the story one doesn't remember. A paradox.

This is where we must operate, not as a scientist but as an artist, not as an archaeologist but as a lover, in fact, as more than a lover.

Picasso once said, "Art is a lie that tells us the truth," and this is the sense in which we must become artist, lover, seducer, and Casanova. As a lure to bringing out the truth we must be willing to invent, to lie a little. Oh, not to ourselves, or even to our readers, but definitely to our brain. It is a creative right-brain strategy that we sometimes need to get past the guard of our critical left brain which, for reasons of its own, is trying to hide the past.

So, as you move from the terra firma of one clear-as-a-bell memory to another equally well-grounded memory, if you suddenly find yourself sinking into the quicksand of no memory, you can regain your footing by simply inventing parts of an episode until the clear memory reappears.

Perhaps you don't like the idea of lying; perhaps this suggestion arouses in you the same enthusiasm that you had for castor oil as a child, curfews as a teenager and boot camp as a young man. "I'm not a person who invents," my students often protest. "If I wanted to write fiction, I would write fiction. I'm here to write my life's stories." This is all quite true. We are not dropping invented artifacts into archaeological digs and trying to pretend they are real—a Piltdown Man approach to life-story writing. Not at all.

Our purpose is to entice the brain into yielding up the truth. So, once we have invented part of the story, we must rely on our intuition to let us know when something feels false, and then to rewrite it, moving toward the truth as best we can.

Occasionally, the brain does not yield what we hope it will. In that case, simply preface the passage with a phrase such as, "As well as I can remember..." or, "My memory is a bit blank here but I think the next part of the story goes something like this..." A disclaimer like that is all you need. No one can then hold you to the facts; you are off the hook. If a question to which you do not know or remember the answer arises in your mind, by all means raise the question and answer it by saying "I don't remember" or "I don't know." If the question comes up, it *must* be answered, even if the answer is simply, "I don't remember." This way the reader will not remain puzzling over the question and ignore the rest of the story.

Here is what our review checklist might look like now:

1. Is my story visual?

2. Does it have emotional impact?

3. Is it told from a consistent point of view?

4. Do the details make the story clearer and more interesting?

5. Does the dialogue help tell the story and make the characters more interesting?

6. Have I kept to one, well-focused incident at a time?

7. Are the characters' qualities evident?

8. Have I created a window through which the action can be seen?

9. Are my feelings about the incident clearly expressed?

10. Does the structure work?

11. Have I improvised toward the facts where my memory has failed?

REWRITING

For those of you who are continually working on rewriting your stories to make them more interesting and more readable, here is an example of how a modest experience can be rewritten to make it tighter and more effective using just a few simple steps:

1. Rearrange some paragraphs so that they start with some dialogue and/or some action.

2. Tighten up the background information and bring it in after the action/dialogue in the beginning.

3. Keep to the spine of the story—our example begins with a goose and ends with a mention of the goose.

THE GOOSE STORY (1)
by Vela Mellus

It was autumn. The leaves were turning red and yellow and it was a perfect day to take two little boys to the Los Angeles Zoo. I'm not familiar with the Zoo now but then there was a barnyard where little children could pet goats and ponies, feed chickens, ducks and geese. They could also see a cow being milked.

2 My daughter and I packed a picnic basket and set off with two eager little boys. We strolled by the bears, tigers and other animals but it wasn't till we got to the barnyard that the boys really became interested and had fun. Here they could come in close contact with the animals.

It was a perfect place to take pictures. How great to snap the children feeding chickens and to get those happy smiles on their faces. I was so busy taking pictures I didn't notice a big, fat goose following me around.

I suddenly felt a hurtful pull and looked to see the goose had a tight grip on my big toe. He had braced his feet, stretched his neck to the last inch, and was hanging on.

1 "I can't believe this," I yelled. "Look, Dede."

"Mother, give him a kick," I heard her yell, as she was having a fit of laughter.

"I can't. He won't let go."

"I'll get a stick," I heard my grandson say.

By this time we were all laughing so hard watching this silly goose.

A few days prior I had fallen in the shower and

1 had broken the toes on my left foot. They were so swollen I couldn't wear a shoe and so was wearing sandals; one toe was so swollen it was white, and to a goose it must have looked like a fat, juicy grub. He finally gave up seeing whether it was going to come off and I went home with all toes intact.

◊ ◊ ◊

Class members laughed, and suggested she start with dialogue or action. Here is her second version.

THE GOOSE STORY (2)

1 "Oh, no. I can't believe this," I yelled, shaking my foot, trying to discourage a big fat goose from trying to eat one of my toes.

"Mother, kick him," I heard my daughter say as she was having a fit of laughter.

"I can't. He won't let go."

"I'll get a stick," My grandson said. "I'll make him let go."

By then we were all laughing so hard to see this silly goose back up, brace himself, stretch his neck to the last inch and hang on.

I had fallen in the shower and the toes on my left foot were broken. I could not wear a shoe and so was wearing sandals—and one toe was so swollen it was white and must have looked like a fat, juicy grub.

2 We were in the barnyard at that time at the Los Angeles Zoo, and the boys were feeding the ducks and chickens, watching a cow being milked, and generally having a great time. It was such a perfect place to take pictures. I was so busy trying to get those happy smiles I didn't notice this goose that was following me until he attacked.

3 My two grandsons had a great day, but what really made the day was the goose.

CHAPTER SIX

WRITING ABOUT
THE INNER YOU

To KNOW WHAT WE ARE FEELING AS EVENTS ARE taking place around us is a very special human capability. Psychologists and psychotherapists spend countless hours helping their clients "get in touch" with themselves, meaning, in part, developing the capacity to become aware of their feelings. You may recall that we discussed this awareness in an earlier chapter. By means of the third eye, we said, we may become aware of our feelings. The ability to transfer these feelings onto paper is what makes us writers. With the desired result that, with the right word, we can penetrate through to a reader's heart.

COMPOSING

We will now discuss in more detail the two kinds of narratives which reveal these feelings. One type describes events and activities in the outside world, which can be seen by many people when and if they are around. The second type is the journey through the inner world of our thoughts and feelings, which can be seen by others only if we bring it out before them with the storyteller's art.

Here is an example of the first type of narrative, which takes place in the outside world.

HOUSES
by Eugene Mallory

The year is 1935. It is a bad year in Iowa. In 1933 the farm industry had no prices. Most commodities were not worth enough to pay the freight to market. Livestock, not worth the little it cost to feed them, roamed the country roads. In 1934 the drought came and very little grew. Prices went up but there was little to sell. Now in 1935 crops are fair but prices are falling like wounded ducks. The whole state, already drained of money, is thinking, "Here we go again."

The place is Lincoln Way, "fraternity row," Ames, Iowa. I have just stopped the car in a spray of flying sand at the curb. Something is wrong. The Chi Phi house, the house that was never dark, is now dark and stares blankly back at me.

Dorothy, my wife of two years, is with me. We are on our way to the house in Hampton were I grew up. We both know at once what must have happened, but neither wishes to say.

The Chi Phi house had been home to me during the years after my mother's death. My father had lain upstairs in the Hampton house, lost in the ruined corridors of his mind. What horrors he found there he could not, or would not say. One look into his eyes made the looker grateful for the silence. I had fled that house as soon as I could, and found refuge here, a second home. Now it, too, is gone.

The Chi Phi alumni had owned this house. A downtown bank had owned the mortgage. The bank had ended in that strange, sad holiday, the bank holiday of 1933. As long as the student residents could generate enough revenue for the alumni to keep up interest and taxes, the house went on. The alumni had made up shortages before, but were too hard-pressed themselves to do so again. The bank liquidators had no choice either. The word was "foreclose." How many dreams and plans and lives, too, had been foreclosed in those bitter years! The word hovers, a chilling presence in the air between us, but we do not speak. I think I can make out the Chi Phi name plate beside the door and say, "I think I can see the name still there. I am going to look." I leave, before a woman's realism can end the faint and futile hope.

Halfway up the wall I am sure the bronze is there. CHI PHI. We did not flash our Greek around. The Greek was reserved for the plain red and gold badge. "Badge, not pin, you clod." I touch the name plate to be sure. The door is locked. It should not be, but unless repaired, the back door cannot be locked.

I go across the lawn and down the steep rutted drive. The flat unpaved lot holds no cars, or does it? There is something at the back. I have a little feeble light. A flash and I recognize the hulk. Stu's ancient and decrepit Auburn Speedster. It had brought him from Chicago in style, but once down the drive it never had the strength to bring itself back up. I turn away, leaving the carcass in its trap.

I head for the kitchen door, pushing aside almost tangible memories. Freddy Wilson's new hat, the endless verses of "God, but it's cold in Iowa." The door yields as I knew it would. The outside air is sharp with cold. Inside, the air is colder still, and lifeless and heavy in the chest. What was in this house? I had met death in that other house, on the days when caskets banked in flowers had stood before the curved glass of the parlor windows and old Mr. Beebe came to leave his card and pay his respects to those whose lives had worn away. That was a house where death had come. What went with death, death and desolation? Desolation has come here.

A verse from scripture I had learned in this house comes slowly back to mind. The Chi Phi founding fathers had used it in the ritual they wrote a hundred years ago. It was natural, since six of the twelve had Reverend before their names: "...the flower of the field flourisheth. The wind passeth over it. The place thereof knows it no more." Indeed, some ancient seed has passed and here it will be no more.

I suddenly realize that, lost in thought, I am wasting my feeble light. Do I need a light to think? I snap it off and soon find that in this place, in this darkness, I do not think so well. The light comes back a little stronger, and I decide to look into the dining room.

Something is crunching underfoot, the Chi Phi china smashed upon the floor. Vandals have been here, the tribe that ravaged Rome. Could they never die?

The huge oval table is still there but my light will hardly reach its length. It has been stripped and only rags of padding cover the naked lumber.

I call back the vision of the last formal dinner I saw here. The small town and country boys sweating in their stiff collars, hard shirt fronts and black bow ties. Our dandy, Meliher, at ease and resplendent in white tie and tails. The girls, bare arms and shoulders gleaming in the candle light. The strapless ones a bit uneasy as to just how much was gleaming.

All so young, rehearsing the glamour and sophistication of the lives they hoped to lead. The vision is hard to hold. The malignant gloom devours the candlelight. My little light is fading too, its battery sucked dry by the darkness and the cold. It is time to go.

When I reach the car, I tell the news, "I got in all right, but they are gone, and the place was vandalized."

Dorothy puts her arms about me and said, "You're shivering Gene. Let's go home."

That car is new and fast. No killing wind can pass over us this night. The Hampton house is home again.

The next time I was on fraternity row, the Chi Phi house was gone and the basement yawned, an open grave. The details of the break-up, I never knew. No one was ever hopeful enough even to write and ask for money.

Money and hope were both in short supply in the Iowa of 1935.

◊ ◊ ◊

You will notice that each object described in this story has an enormous past. When such an object is described effectively, it can have a strong emotional impact on the reader or listener. This concept is similar in many ways to one of the exercises used by actors trained in the Stanislavski system, called "circumstances surrounding an object." In this exercise, the actor builds a past life around an object so that, when it is used on stage or on film, the audience will see and feel the connections to the past—the happy, sad, poignant memories connected with the object.

To given an example from my own life, the interior of the car I own, a 1964 Volvo, has a wonderful smell to it. It is a distinctive smell, one which everyone who climbs into the car notices. But only I know that it is a smell almost identical to my father's Packard, a car I loved, a smell which reminds me of a happy time in my life when I was small and my father was alive and showing me things in and around Detroit, things which I saw and experienced for the first time.

Expressing inner emotion

The second type of narrative is that in which an event in the outside world triggers a flood of inner feelings, often conflicting ones. As with non-objective paintings such as those of Kandinsky or Jackson Pollock, the emotions may become detached from the object which inspired them. Or there may continue to be some reference to the object. In the late paintings of artists such as J.M.W. Turner (*The Fighting Téméraire, The Morning After the Deluge*) and Claude Monet (*Water Lilies*), there is always a hint of the object in the abstract swirls of emotion on the canvas.

Occasionally, the emotions of the inner world rise to the surface and reappear as part of the outer world in a surprising and revealing portrait of the writer's own emotional landscape. As an example of this please read Rose Rothenberg's story, "Young Love" (page 75).

As the reader can see, it is a fascinating glimpse into the writer's inner emotions, first experienced as though her pain is very close to us. We also see the outer world, represented by her brother, quite far away as if glimpsed through a tunnel. By the end of the story she has come to the end of the tunnel; her brother and his world are now experienced as very close to us and her emotions have softened. She has returned to the land of the living.

The stories you have just read are fine examples of a strong awareness of emotions being part of the subject of the narrative. In "Houses" the objects are so filled with emotion that we, the readers, feel that emotion as well. In "Young Love" the writer's emotions are the subject of the story, and we feel her pain as she struggles to return to normal feelings, a struggle we have all experienced at one time or another.

Here, then, are the four steps to follow when writing from within.

1. Follow all the steps you have already taken to set clearly in your mind a story or incident which you would like to narrate.

2. Review the story or incident which is in your mind, recollecting how you felt with each turn of events during the story.

3. Recall not only your emotions and those of any other central character, but also how other, very specific people around you responded to the situation.

4. Allow yourself to make your own emotions— your sadness, pain, awe, amusement, fascination, etc. —the subject of certain episodes.

◊ ◊ ◊

This discussion and these stories may have triggered in you a memory or a story you may wish to write. If so, climb back into that easy chair and return to the place of distant memory...

REVIEWING

In reviewing your story at this point, you may ask

yourself: Is it unfolding naturally and easily, and are the emotional responses of the central character, the writer and others also quite clear?

And to our checklist we now add one final item: the presence of the writer's own emotions as the subject of his or her life's stories.

1. Is my story visual

2. Does it have emotional impact?

3. Is it told from a consistent point of view—a child's perhaps?

4. Do the details make the story clearer and more interesting?

5. Does the dialogue help tell the story and make the characters more interesting?

6. Have I kept to one, well-focused incident at a time?

7. Are the characters' qualities evident?

8. Have I set the stage so the action can be seen?

9. Are my feelings about the incident clearly expressed?

10. Does the structure work?

11. Have I improvised toward the facts where my memory has failed?

12. Are my own emotions the subject of any stories?

REWRITING

You now have the techniques you need to write your life stories, to express your inner feelings as well as describe people and events in the outside world. In your subsequent stories, try to achieve an effective balance of narration, dialogue and inner monologue. Not every story requires such a balance but most stories will be enhanced by it. And remember to use your inner thoughts and feelings, to write from within.

In Part II we will move on to writing about experiences of adulthood. The same techniques apply to writing stories from these phases of life. These stories will come naturally, if not easily, when you have completed the stories and exercises in Part I. As a conclusion to this part, let me emphasize again the importance of writing your earliest memory, and of writing from a child's point of view: these are the exercises that will develop your roots as a writer, and will allow you to find your authentic voice.

PART TWO

WRITING
THE SIGNIFICANT MOMENTS
IN YOUR LIFE

CHAPTER SEVEN

LIFE STAGES
AND THE JOURNEY

Y̶OU NOW HAVE A WEALTH OF WRITING
techniques at your fingertips and, after several
weeks, perhaps months, of working on your memoirs,
have probably recorded quite a few memories from your
childhood.

In fact, you probably have as much technique as
you will ever need. Oh, your style will improve as you
learn to edit your work more carefully, and your
dialogue will become sharper as you listen closely to the
conversations of those around you (try not to be too obvious when you are listening!). But, all in all, you have
the basic techniques you need.

Now you are ready to take on more complicated experiences. The memories of childhood are so powerful
that they form wonderful stories almost by themselves.
On the other hand, adult life is rather like a vast sea. A
few things really stand out but, mostly, our life is a

series of larger and smaller ripples that spread out around us as we move in different directions.

The decision to write one's life's stories is a decision to embark on a voyage of recollection and rediscovery, to find the things that really moved and affected us, and shaped our lives. As we voyage over and across this sea we will encounter markers of those experiences, and special memories will bubble up to the surface. In particular, there are those things we experienced for the first time: romance, work, war, marriages, children, career highs and lows, second careers, retirement, a loved one's death.

These act as powerful anchor buoys for our writing, not only as places to begin our narratives but also as markers on which to set our sights. Some lives are especially tumultuous, filled with waves, and these markers help such people find out where to begin crossing the sea of their life.

For most of you, revisiting these memories will be painful as well as joyous, consuming as well as satisfying. But remember that revisiting a painful past may be the most therapeutic thing you can do for yourself. By putting the experience on paper, reading it aloud and hearing your words, you can begin to let go of it. Or perhaps we could say that it will let go of you.

At the same time, the incidents may show themselves to be part of a larger narrative, and will take on a different meaning for you. You will begin to see patterns of different kinds occurring in your life, and these incidents may become part of that pattern.

Perhaps, in all honesty, you view your life as a failure. You may find that an accurate retelling of the first episode of this failure could lead to a reconciliation with relatives and friends whom you long ago alienated in some way. Or perhaps you were headed in a dull, ordinary or pedestrian direction when one of these "firsts" occurred, redirecting your life in some way, and now you understand the meaning and value of the experience.

Virtually every religion on this earth has, at its center, a person who has undergone a journey of some kind, who has been through a number of trials and emerged on the other side in some way transformed or reborn. That heroic journey, so well chronicled by mythologist Joseph Campbell, is not the sole province of great or important men and women. In one way or another we are all embarked on our life's journey, are tested by life, and have the opportunity to be reborn at some point. Some of us will experience this rebirth in the process of writing our life's stories, because only then will our lives make sense.

Two important areas of experience we will need to review are our relationships with our parents and with our children. Often, these relationships have not been entirely happy or, particularly in the case of our children, we may feel the process is not complete. Nevertheless, we need to address these experiences as directly as possible. We have related many experiences from childhood in earlier stories; now, it is time to speak to our parents directly. Experience has shown that once we say what we need to say to our parents, then we can say what we need to say to our children. This is not easy to do, but the rewards are immense.

All of this is preparation for the ultimate experience we face: death. Most of us are fearful about death. We envision a state where our faculties have diminished with age, our loved ones may be gone, and we are alone. But that is only one way of viewing death. There are other ways, and we will come back to them in a later chapter.

At this point you may want to return to your family's past and write something about your parents and grandparents as an introduction to your memoirs. If you wish to write more detailed stories of your family's past, see Chapter Thirteen, "Other Stories," and read Lucy MacDougall's "Family History (3)" (page 143). When you feel you are ready, look out toward that magnificent sea, step down into the boat of memory and journey to the first buoy in sight: first love.

CHAPTER EIGHT

FIRST LOVE

AT FIRST GLANCE, ONE MIGHT THINK THAT describing a first love is no particular problem. "She/he was very beautiful/handsome and nice and I just fell in love." Unfortunately, such a description has a problem—it doesn't really let the reader in on what the lover thought and felt. How do we go about letting the reader in on this experience? There are two qualities which are worth noting in most stories of first love. Something has changed in the life of the narrator, something which allows love to enter for the first time, which makes the narrator vulnerable to love's arrow. This quality appears and reappears in many stories of first love, and may also appear in yours. If so, be aware of this new twist to your life.

The second quality is related to our earlier discussions about the "third eye." We find ourselves recording what is going on inside us as well as recording what is happening in the outside world. The ingredients of this awareness are, in no particular order, a description of our first love, a description of the incident or incidents in which the two of us participated, and then a description of how we felt while participating in the experience. What makes most stories of first love unusual is the sense that, although there is an objective world out there, when love enters—or leaves—the scene, everything, including the self and perhaps the world, is transformed by a new chemistry, a heightened awareness, as though one has taken a drug of some kind.

In the story which follows the writer captures the extremes of feeling— both high and low—which sometimes accompany the experience of first love.

YOUNG LOVE
by Rose Rothenberg

The spring day dawned sunny and bright. The blue of the sky stretched endlessly without cloud interruption. But the day's brilliance could not penetrate my blanket of grayness. I hugged it close to me as I had for days since emerging from the black hole of nothingness to contemplate the bleakness of the new world I had entered.

The shell of my being functioned still in the old world. In the aliveness of this world my shell lived, slept, ate, interacted with family and friends. My true self secreted itself in darkness, wrapped itself in solitary unfeeling grayness. It resisted all efforts to puncture the layers of cloud matter that swirled around me and protected me from hurt.

I alone knew where I was and why—or so I thought. One evening as my shell walked silently beside my brother, he thought to reach me in the colorless beyond where I had escaped, to pull me out into the sunshine with him. "There's more than one fish in the sea," he said.

My shell responded in the flippant way of that

other world. "I never did like fish anyway. They can all stay in the sea so far as I'm concerned. Try your psychology on someone else." And I marched angrily ahead.

My brother, three and a half years my senior, confident at twenty-two in his role of big brother and protector, shrugged his shoulders and snorted, "Forget it—it's not worth being in the dumps about anyway."

My shell and he continued on our way but my suffering soul retreated further into the comforting void.

There came a time when my true self lifted the protective curtain that enveloped me and peered into the world I had left. The glare and brightness of that place was too intense to be faced, and quickly I dropped the gray curtain once more—until the next time.

As time passed I lifted the curtain more boldly and was able to absorb the otherworldly brightness for longer periods. Inevitably there came a day when I flung the heavy grayness aside completely and met and merged with my shell. Together and inseparably we walked once more in the warm sunshine.

I knew then for certain that my first love, my deep youthful love, my rejected love, would not be my last love.

◊ ◊ ◊

First love often places demands, not only on the person in love but on everyone else around. When writing your own story of first love, see if you can recollect what effect the turmoil in your life and heart had on those around you. Since most of us are not going to experience first love again, we can only hope that those who come after us will have a grandmother as understanding as the one in this next story.

ADVICE TO A FOOLISH VIRGIN
by Bess Shapiro

I'm deeply in love with Bill. I'm also deeply in lust with Bill. I have just reached my twentieth birthday. My heart is ready, and my body is clamoring for that mysterious consummation that will bind us together forever.

But where can that magic take place?

I share a bedroom with Grandma. I complain to her, after assuring her that she's the dearest roommate a girl could have.

"Dammit, Grandma! I don't have any privacy. What if I want to make a baby with Bill?"

Grandma gives me a sly smile. "Foolish little girl! Just say to me, 'Grandma, take a walk!' How long does it take to make a baby? Five minutes."

◊ ◊ ◊

So, perhaps you feel it is time for you to return to your place of memory. Find your comfortable spot, close your eyes, recollect your past, and write...

Chapter Nine

Young Adulthood:
A Time Of Decision

As we look out over the vast sea of our life's experiences, past the marker buoys of childhood memories and first love, we can see one coming up called, perhaps, "first freedom" or "memories of young adulthood."

It is a time when the dependent years of childhood have ended. The first significant phase of education is complete. For some, it means a high school diploma; for others who have worked from an early age, it means some skills have been acquired. It is the first time in our lives we are able to say, "I want to do such-and-such," and can expect to be free to pursue our goals and desires despite any lingering strictures of societal convention, self-expectation and parental authority.

For some people it is a time of frustration, of decisions made unconsciously and later regretted: a college chosen hastily, a marriage and a family formed unwisely. For others it is a time of adolescent confusion. See Isidore Ziferstein's "Fessex, Fessex, Prenez Garde!" (page 217) for a charming portrayal of young Isidore's struggles between loyalty to his friends and the call of his hormones.

In our memoirs we must honestly acknowledge how we felt about ourselves then and how we feel about these decisions today. In every case there were probably other choices which may have seemed like no choice at the time. For example, to have been drafted into the army may have seemed inevitable in 1942 for a male high school graduate in good physical condition, but many volunteered for other branches of the armed forces or were involved in the war effort in different ways or even left the country in protest. So as you sit down to write your memoirs of this very significant period of early freedom, recapture for yourself that mental/physical energy you had, as well as the feelings and emotions which surrounded the choices you made.

This period of young adulthood is also a time of hilarious, high adventure. The experiences into which we enter, willingly or not, often yield hysterically funny stories, as we battle against convention, expectation and authority.

I would like you now to sit back and enjoy one young man's struggle with the U.S. Army in the days before Pearl Harbor. (This story precedes the "Jefferson Barracks, Missouri" story that starts on page 30 and is continued in Selection Seven.)

THREE PENNSYLVANIA PATRIOTS
by John Strong

Bill Bee, Ford Smith and I, (Big) John Strong, enlisted in the United States Army, October 15, 1940, at Indiana, Pennsylvania. Our coal-mining home town, Clymer, was nine miles away. Indiana was the county seat, and the town where actor Jimmy Stewart was raised. His dad had a hardware store there.

We had read that if you enlisted before the impending draft, you could chose your army branch and even the location of the post you wished. This appealed to us, and besides, we were very patriotic young men.

The army had an unsavory reputation in 1940—drunkards, shiftless fellows and so on. Well, we three God-fearing fellows would soon change that, we thought.

I bumped into Mr. Davis, my former high school principal, as I was about to enter the recruiting building. "I'm going to enlist in the U.S. Army, Mr. Davis," I replied proudly.

"What, in there with all those b——," he started to say "bums," but didn't.

"If I enlist, I can pick my branch and station," I explained. "Furthermore, I know that soon we will be in the war raging in Europe, and I may as well get a rating now."

Mr. Davis didn't agree. "We won't be in the war. You go back to college. Get your degree and start teaching history and coaching, John."

"Maybe, after I get back, Mr. Davis," I replied.

"You were a good student and a fine athlete, John. I know you are making a mistake, but anyway—good luck, let's keep in touch!" With that he walked around the corner, glancing back just before he disappeared.

Before Bill, Ford and I entered the building, Ford said, "I have about fifteen decayed teeth. The black parts look like fillings, so that's the way I'm going to pass the test."

It sounded impossible to me, but, by gosh, it worked. I found out later that Ford could think up good ideas like this on the spur of the moment.

To begin with, the sergeant doing the examination wasn't too particular. He wanted every candidate to pass. Ford maneuvered the sergeant under dim light, then opened his mouth.

"Are all those dark parts of your teeth fillings or decayed spots?" he asked.

"All fillings, just had them done, so I could pass the exam—cost over a hundred to do it," replied Ford confidently.

The sergeant looked over at Ford with a quizzical eye, then said, "OK, I'll take your word for it—all fillings."

We three passed all the tests at the physical examination. Got our papers and were now waiting for the bus to Harrisburg, Pennsylvania, where we would be sworn in. The sergeant gave me the papers.

"You're in charge, Big Soldier." I felt somewhat important at this first assignment.

As we sat on a waiting bench at the bus stop, I got thinking about Bob McTavish. He had been two years behind us in high school, was a good athlete—a tall fellow. Bob had just gotten out of the army after a three-year tour of duty. I had talked with Bob a few days ago. He told me that I was foolish to enlist—a bunch of rough guys in there. The only two things he learned in the army was how to box and how to drink. He never had touched a drop before he enlisted.

Bob prided himself on knocking out Sgt. Olson, of Toledo, Ohio, for the Heavyweight Crown of the Hawaiian Islands. He told me that when he got to drinking hard he thought that he would fight the Swede again.

Another thing he told me was that if I did enlist, "Don't let them send you to Sitka, Alaska, in the Engineer Corps. It's so damned cold and they have you digging in frozen ground and eating fish. The only women are big, burly, pigeon-toed Eskimos." All this was told to Bob by a corporal who had been up there.

Eventually, the bus pulled in and we went on board. Just as the bus started to leave, a voice sounded off, "Don't go yet—another enlistee." Our eyes moved to the front door of the bus. Who should stumble in, drunker than a wino, but Bob McTavish, the fellow I had just been thinking about. He was the one who had warned me about never enlisting. The sergeant had probably taken Bob even though he surely didn't know he was enlisting.

Bob staggered to where I was sitting, spied the empty seat beside me and flopped down. At the same time, he grabbed the papers from my hands.

"They said a Big Guy, meaning you, had the papers and was in charge. Well, you aren't any longer. I was a corporal and now I'm in charge," he announced, slurring his words.

Soon Bob was asleep, leaning on my shoulder and snoring like a buzz saw all the way into Harrisburg, a 175-mile ride.

We were fed at a sorry-looking restaurant with strictly second class food, then taken to a skid row type hotel. I couldn't believe the poor condition of the dump. There were big holes in the wall so you could see right into the next bedroom. Cockroaches raced around the baseboards, emulating Indianapolis. In addition, there were two men in a bed. Whom did I draw? That's right—Bob McTavish, still semi-drunk.

Finally falling to sleep, I was rudely awakened by a blow on my Adam's apple. How that hurt! Then there were three blows to my head, chest and shoulders. "Take that, you Dirty Swede," Bob was yelling.

I tried to tie up Bob's arms, but no luck. Finally, I jumped out of bed. "Bob, you aren't fighting the Swede, it's me, John," I shouted as I pulled on the dim light.

He looked at me with a dazed stare, then fell back in bed and went to sleep. I stayed awake a while watching the cockroaches racing. I was betting on the one with the white dot on his back—he won!

I noticed through the hole in the wall that in the next room a table stood near the hole, a bottle of booze rested on the table. The two recruits from Scranton, Pennsylvania, had bought it for some snorts, probably to forget the lousy hotel.

No sooner did I fall asleep in bed than I heard a banging on the door. It was the Scranton duo from the next room. I jumped out of bed and yelled, "What do you want?"

"We want our bottle of Jack Daniels, that's what we want—just bought it. That big drunk in there reached through the hole and stole it."

Sure enough, that was true. He must have taken it when he went to the toilet. The bottle was near Bob's side of the bed and it was practically empty.

I handed the bottle to one of the guys, who moaned, "An empty bottle—the dirty drunk took our expensive whiskey."

The next morning we were assembled into a huge room and sworn into the U.S. Army. The officer who swore us in was a West Pointer in street clothing. Imagine that! Robert E. Lee, U. S. Grant and Stonewall Jackson were not sworn in by an officer in civilian clothes—not by any means!

Then the Big Operation began—assignments! A tall, thin captain sounding like a tobacco auctioneer rattled off the requisitions coming in: "Four men, Quartermaster, Canal Zone. You four reading magazines by the door. You are going to Panama.

Three men, field artillery, Fort Meade, Maryland—you three sitting over there," he pointed. "Six men, Medical corps, Puerto Rico. You six standing by the radiator."

And so it went. This couldn't be true. We enlisted to pick our branch and location of station, and here this captain was sending men in bunches. They probably don't want us all over the world. Why aren't the fellows doing some griping? Why are they taking it so calmly? I don't get it.

Just then the Captain's voice sang out. "One man, Engineering Corps, Sitka, Alaska. You, Big Fellow in that big lounge chair." I couldn't believe it—it was Bob McTavish, sweating out his hangover, Bob, who had told me never to go to Sitka because it was so cold and you dig, dig, dig in the frozen ground, told me about the fish and the burly women—and now Bob was being sent there. Boy, will he be burning mad when he sobers up!

Well, I had enough of this. I told Bob and Ford that when the Captain yells out for three men somewhere in the U.S.A., preferably the Signal Corps or the Air Corps, I would jump up and volunteer the three of us before he could point one out. We didn't want Puerto Rico, Alaska or the Canal Zone. Bill and Ford agreed.

"Three men, Air Corps, Jefferson Barracks, Missouri." Before the Captain could continue, I was on top of him. He looked disappointed that he couldn't point to some guys and send them to a place and branch they didn't want.

So that's how we got our assignment to Jefferson Barracks—what army efficiency!

◊ ◊ ◊

You notice that this memoir of John's is filled with moments of decisive action, often viewed with a wry, tongue-in-cheek humor. For a continuation of John Strong's adventures in the army please turn to the story "Jefferson Barracks, Missouri" (page 187).

Now it is your turn. Roll back the pages of the past to the time when you stood on the brink of young adulthood about to be thrust out into a wider world than you had known before. Sit back in that easy chair, perhaps thumb through some old photo albums or newspapers of a time when you were in your late teens. When you are ready, close your eyes, recollect your past, and write.

CHAPTER TEN

"RIGHT YOU ARE
IF YOU THINK YOU ARE"

YOU MAY HAVE NOTICED AS YOU CIRCLE THE
markers of the important events in your life that
they look different, depending on how far away from
them you are, what light is shining on them, how fast
you are approaching or leaving them, and so on. These
markers will also appear different to others who may
have shared the experience in one or another way.

DIFFERING POINTS OF VIEW

We all know that few events are ever experienced
or remembered the same by any two people. For this exercise, find an event or experience which left a strong
impression on you, one which you are certain a close
relative or friend of yours viewed quite differently. Cor-
respond with your relative or friend, get some agreement about the event you are recollecting, then each of

you write about it. Exchange versions, compare them, then write a commentary about the similarities and differences. My guess is that this task will result in a lot of laughs or may lead to a great deal more understanding of certain episodes involving yourself and this close relative or friend.

The stories below describe a birthday party experienced very differently by two sisters, aged eight and thirteen.

MEMORIES OF A
THIRTEENTH BIRTHDAY PARTY
by Carol Cunningham

My sister Barbara is really a teenager today. Thirteen. She got to have her party last Saturday night. It lasted until eleven o'clock. All the girls got to wear long dresses and the boys had to wear ties. Mom let me go to the party, but I didn't get to wear a long dress. I wish I could have. In a long dress I would have looked older and maybe they wouldn't have treated me like they did.

Everything was so beautiful. Mom had the dining room table all set with flowers and candles and place cards. The place cards were fun. Mom wrote a poem on the place card about everyone who came and then they had to read the poems and figure out which one was about them. Barbara's best friend, Edith, was the easiest. She looks like Betty Grable and the poem said so. Everyone knew where Edith was supposed to sit.

◊ ◊ ◊

MEMORIES OF A
THIRTEENTH BIRTHDAY PARTY
by Barbara Lewis

My sister has asked me to tell you about my thirteenth birthday party. Let's see—it's not easy, as I've managed to block out most of my childhood memories in which "she" was involved, the reason being when I was five years old (and up until that time, the only child, the center of my parents' universe) "she" was brought home. I was a blonde, curly-headed charmer and "she" looked like an abandoned Indian papoose who did nothing but lie there and cry. For years I tried unsuccessfully to get rid of her and as "she" grew, "she" became more impossible. My parents assured me that "she" was my real sister, but she was unbelievably skinny, had long, dark, stringy hair that never looked combed and she collected ghastly paper flowers, also junk of all sorts, which "she" managed to wear somewhere on her person. I was sure that everyone thought we had adopted a gypsy waif.

Anyway, "she" was forced on me relentlessly so at my thirteenth birthday party, there was no escape. "She" was to be included and no amount of crying and threatening would budge my parents. The party was a sit-down dinner and dance. All day my mother (who was a marvelous cook) and the maid cleaned and prepared wonderful dishes, the aromas promising great things to eat. At long last it was time for guests to arrive. Guess who was the first to answer the doorbell? "She," of course, greeting my friends, looking for all the world as though the caravan had forgotten her. I could hardly get a word in. Finally everyone arrived. Jean, whose mother was a best-selling author; Edith, whose father owned a chocolate factory; Elenita, my closest friend, who lived across the street in a large mansion surrounded by high walls; Jerry, whom I don't remember very well; Robert, a tall, good-looking German who went to the American School; and Jim, the blond, handsome athlete. We all attended the American School in Monterrey, Mexico. I had been trying to decide whether Robert or Jim was going to be my boyfriend. Whoever responded the most favorably at the party would be the one.

My mother had written poems about each guest; there was one at each place setting and they were to guess which poem identified which guest. My friends were delighted with the descriptions Mother had given them. Dinner over, it was time to dance. My parents went next door. I quickly turned off several lights so there would be a more romantic atmosphere. We picked out records to be played and started dancing. "She" was right there in the middle of the group, embarrassing me, dancing by herself. I had had great plans for dancing cheek to cheek, maybe a kiss or two, but there "she" was, dancing as though "she" were thirteen and belonged. I had to do something... An inspiration!!! Lock her in the closet; so we did. What a chore it was getting her in there with all the kicking and screaming. I don't think "she" was in there too long, but we were able to dance cheek to cheek and there was some kissing. I also decided Jim was to be my boyfriend. The details are fuzzy as to what happened after "she" was let out. All in all, my party was a success.

"She" is still thin, "she" is still a bit of a gypsy, and her hair would be straight without a permanent. However, "she" is creative, warm, and totally endearing. My closest friend—my sister.

◊ ◊ ◊

In reflecting about the episode you wish to record, you may conclude that one of the stories you've already written would do just fine. If that is the case, then by all means get in touch with the person who may have experienced this episode differently.

If you wish to begin a new story, remember that one of your objectives is to renew or revive an old relationship, so it is best to tread lightly if the subject is at all controversial or painful. But do not be reluctant to share your feelings as you remember them. If you are ready to begin writing once again, then now is the time...

CHAPTER ELEVEN

TRAUMA

SCANNING THE COURSE OF OUR VOYAGE through life, we come to a marker that looks quite different from the others. Although we are looking directly at it, it remains in darkness, as if in perpetual shadows. A strange marker, yet a vital one to our narrative. If we look into ourselves, we realize that the marker has a name written on it, a name that is difficult and painful to read, scrawled at an angle where we can barely see it: TRAUMA

That name gives us a chilly clue to the experiences which lie beneath. Perhaps we would like to pass it by, but we must not.

These traumas may be genuine tragedies, intensely experienced, maybe even caused by ourselves. Now is the time for us to view them clear-sightedly. Most often, they will be the untimely deaths of people we love. Often, too, they may be shocking injuries to someone we love, or even to ourselves. When writing about these experiences, there are four things we must do.

First, we must prepare for reliving the experience and writing about it; just as an athlete goes into training, we must go into training. And just as a part of the training and conditioning is mental—"psyching up" for the task, visualizing good things happening—so we must encourage ourselves by congratulating ourselves, telling ourselves what a good person we are for doing this.

Second, we must finish the story once we have started it. Despite the tears and pain, we must keep writing.

Third, we need to maintain our objectivity, and not blame anyone. As the writer, our job is to make the reader see the truth, to describe to the reader what we see and experience and feel, so that the reader goes through that pain or feeling or experience.

Fourth, we need to resist the temptation to editorialize or moralize about what has happened. We are storytellers; we need to tell stories. Sometimes, at the end of a tragic or traumatic experience, we do come to certain conclusions about the way the universe operates. If this happens to us, it is appropriate to say something. And it is perfectly all right to express confusion and bewilderment at the nature and power of the Creator of us all. But keep it real. One honest observation is worth more than all the platitudes in the world.

◊ ◊ ◊

These four points will help you through remembering and writing this painful episode among your life's stories.

Here are two such experiences written by our writers. You may wish to look closely at them to see if they implement the four suggestions given above, and whether each story is helped by them.

THE SHOCK
by Maxine Freedman

I was married in March of 1929 at the age of sixteen. It took place in St. Louis where I was born. Immediately, we left to live in Columbus, Ohio.

My wonderful young husband had a sister whom we were to live with just after our marriage. She was a devoted sister and loved her brother very much. She resented me for marrying her brother. She disliked me immediately because I wasn't from a wealthy family and not college material. That is what she wanted for her brother. I was not permitted to sit on her living room furniture or feel free in her home.

At that time I had been married four months and was pregnant three months. Sadie, my husband's sister, never suspected that, until I began vomiting and became very sick. She was horrified because she had plans for me to get a job as a salesgirl. Well, I tried to get a job, but not having any experience, it was impossible. Since I could not get a job, Sadie put me to work as her maid in her home, scrubbing floors, washing clothes by hand and ironing all in the basement. Besides, we had to pay her $15.00 a week for room and board. My husband only earned $18.00 a week selling shoes. After one very bad, sick morning, I looked up to see Sadie staring at me.

"Look Maxine, you should see Dr. Levy right away," she said chewing on her lip.

"I don't like doctors and I have never been to one," I replied, getting to my feet and taking a drink of water. "I thought it was too early to be checked by a doctor."

"We will go and visit him," she answered without looking at me. "He was a friend's doctor. You will like him."

"I don't like doctors. I don't want to go!"

"You absolutely have to go," she said, raising her voice. "He can help you so much. Since you and my brother have to earn money, you can't sit around here all day doing nothing. I'll make an appointment to see him; you must get an abortion. Get rid of it. He has done a lot of my friends. There is really nothing to it. No pain. In a few days you will be fine. Just go talk to him, see what he says."

The day came for Sadie and me to visit Dr. Levy. We climbed the steps in his dirty hallway into a small office upstairs. There he was smiling at us. A quack doctor if ever I saw one. He took me to his examining room and Sadie followed. She pushed me onto the examining table. It happened so fast... Dr. Levy started to abort me. I screamed, so Sadie put a handkerchief in my mouth and held my shoulders down. It was over. I remember calling the doctor some terrible names like, "Murderer!"

"Get her out of here quick!" he said to Sadie. "I don't want anyone to hear her."

As I staggered to the outer office, I saw my husband waiting for me. I couldn't believe that this was planned. He had left his job to take me home. He helped me down the stairway to a waiting cab. There was no conversation between us. I was in excruciating pain. In a few minutes we were home. Sadie came to my room with a green plant. I screamed at her and told her never to come near me again.

That night I lost my baby. Jack saw it in the bathroom and later told me it was a girl. I fell asleep crying bitterly. It was a terrible shock to me. Several weeks later I recuperated from that experience. I have never forgotten it.

I did not want to live in Sadie's house anymore. Shortly after that we moved in with the people next door and paid the same amount that we paid Sadie.

Living in this new and strange house was unbearable to me. I was always alone and never had anyone to talk to until my husband came home at night. Living in a strange city and not having any friends or family, all I wanted was to leave Columbus and go back to St. Louis.

One afternoon there was a knock at the door. It was my mother. She had found out where we were living. I said, "Mama, please take us home with you to St. Louis. I am so unhappy living with strangers." I never told her what had happened to me about losing the baby. It was secret for life.

So we went home to St. Louis with Mama. It was such a joyful bus ride. Mama was so happy to have us back with her—Jack, Mama and me going back to St. Louis. Mama kept holding my hand and also holding her dentures to keep them from falling out of her mouth as it was a very bumpy ride all the way home.

◊ ◊ ◊

THE VISIT
by Lily De Lauder

Many times over the years, I've tried to replay that day in my mind. At best, it's a dim, confusing recollection, mingled with a haunting sadness.

It was early morning when Mama told me we were going to Uncle Johnny's house. I was elated by the promise of a visit with my favorite uncle, but Mama was in a strange mood, distant—almost hostile. When I held up my pink voile dress for her approval, she snatched it from me. "No! Not that! Have some sense, child. Here—it's cold—wear this." She handed me a heavy, navy wool dress which I detested. It was a "hand-me-down" from my sister,

Cathy.

I was five years old and knew better than to dis-
agree with Mama. As I buttoned the neck of the ugly
dress and felt the coarse fabric on my arms, I
blinked back the tears. Uncle Johnny loved the pink
one. Whenever he saw me wearing it he would smile
and say, "Here comes my little strawberry bon-bon
with the gingerbread hair." The teasing about my
red hair didn't bother me when it came from him.
He was Mama's brother and his hair was the same
color as mine; it was a family trait.

To me, my uncle was Superman, Sir Galahad and
Prince Charming, all rolled into one; I adored him!
He was the one person who seemed to understand
my shyness and, instinctively, knew how to help me
overcome it. In retrospect, I believe that, as a child,
he may have had the same feelings of fear and sen-
sitivity that I had.

Occasionally, Mama mentioned Uncle Johnny's
wife and two children (boys) but I didn't recall meeting them. Whenever he came, he came alone and
unexpectedly. He always wore a fresh white shirt
and bright green tie. His auburn hair would be neat-
ly brushed, and his blue eyes smiled constantly.

One day, he offered me a bright, silver sixpence.
I refused although we were poor and sixpence was
a tidy sum to a five-year-old. Then he searched his
pockets and found a shiny new penny. "Look," he
said in a grave voice, "this must be yours, it's the
same color as your hair! Here," he said, handing it
to me, "that's your happy penny."

Now it was almost noon and Mama finally said
it was time to leave. I'd never known a morning to
go so slowly. It had been several weeks since I'd seen
my favorite uncle. One day I'd heard my parents
talking about him and a hospital was named. When
I asked if he was ill, they said something vague

which sounded like T.B. I sensed something was wrong, but was much too young to understand.

I remember how he'd helped me a few months earlier when I was grieving for my pet puppy, Chip. Chip was ill, and Mama told me to put him in a box and take him to the animal shelter. On the way back, I felt as though I'd not only lost my pet but also betrayed him. Nobody seemed to care, but Uncle Johnny did! He took me to a nearby park where he let me feed the ducks and birds. He, too, loved animals and knew I was heartbroken.

Just before Mama and I left the house, I got out an old tea caddy which was my "treasure box." I took out the penny and put it deep into the pocket of the dark dress. Then I took a glossy postcard which Mama had bought for me in Blackpool, a nearby resort. It was a picture of a beautiful lady with long, auburn curls. She wore a green satin dress and held a gold mirror. Uncle Johnny would like this!

At last, we were on the bus; it was crowded and stuffy. Mama was even quieter than usual. She carried a paper bag with string handles; occasionally, she took a large, white handkerchief from it and held it to her face. Wound around her fingers were black rosary beads, which she touched frequently without looking at them.

I was glad she had worn her "good" coat, dark maroon with a leopard-skin collar. Her soft, brown hair was braided and pinned, wreath-like, under a tiny, black hat. She was a slim, pretty woman with a look of constant pensiveness. I often wondered why she was always sad. I wanted to talk to her, to hold her, but she seemed aloof and preoccupied.

We got off the bus and started to walk. I offered to carry the bag, which seemed heavy. She shook her head, looking straight ahead. Suddenly she stopped and, reaching down, took my hand. Her eyes softened and her mouth was almost smiling. "Be a good girl, Lily Ann," she said quietly. "Don't be asking questions."

I nodded. "Yes Mama. I just want to see Uncle Johnny."

The neighborhood was poor, with endless rows of drab, gray-brown houses. Children played hop-scotch and jump-rope on the narrow sidewalks; they turned to look at us as we went by.

Mama's grip on my hand tightened as we stopped at one of the houses. The door was opened by a short, heavy-set woman wearing a long dress, the same color as her dark brown hair. "Sarah," Mama said, "this is Lily Ann, my youngest."

The woman looked down at me, her eyes cold. "Sure. I've heard tell of her. I'm your aunt, Sarah Hart. I'm Johnny's wife." She turned abruptly and we followed her through a dark hallway into a room filled with people.

In the center of the room was a large table covered by a long, white linen tablecloth. Mama took a casserole dish from the bag and placed it with the rest of the food on the cluttered table. Then she sat down, silent. The rosary beads were still coiled around her slim fingers.

In vain, I looked for my uncle. The people in the room were gathered in small groups, eating and talking; they were strangers to me. Finally I summoned the courage to ask. "Mama, I want to see Uncle Johnny." I held up the postcard, "I brought him something." She gave me a confused look, then took my hand.

"Listen, love." Her voice was gentle and I noticed how pretty her eyes were. "I want you to remember, your uncle's been poorly for a long time." She looked away, I sensed it was difficult for her to speak.

She led me back through the hallway into another room, the parlor. It was a dark, musty room, sparsely furnished. Beside the long window, which was covered by cream lace curtains, was a large, trunk-like object. As Mama left, I glanced around then walked over to it. It looked like my beloved uncle but it *wasn't* him—I knew that. The white face and shroud exaggerated the red hair. There was no smile on the tired face; it was a cruel caricature.

In a confused way, I knew Uncle Johnny was dead but could not fully grasp it. I wanted to run and keep on running, away from Mama and all those strange people. I walked back through the hallway, feeling as though I was trapped in a nightmare.

Through the doorway of the crowded room, I could see the people still eating and talking. "Such a pity," a large, red-faced woman was saying. "Poor chap was only thirty-two."

Slowly, as though in a dream, I found my way back to the parlor. Reaching into the deep pocket of my dress, I took out the postcard. Placing it inside the casket, I looked at the lifeless figure. "Uncle Johnny—I brought you something." Then, as I tightly clutched the "happy penny," I whispered, "I love you."

I sat on the edge of a small, wooden chair, and watched the reflection of the votive candle flickering on the faded wallpaper.

Suddenly I felt lost and weary. He was gone—my friend and counselor whom I loved so much. This was the visit I'd looked forward to so eagerly.

"Lily Ann." The voice seemed to come from far away. It was Mama, kneeling beside me. She put her arm around my shoulders, "Uncle Johnny knows you love him. I do too...he was special." We held each other close. It was the first time I'd seen Mama cry.

◊ ◊ ◊

Now it is time for you to look into the waters beneath that shadowy marker and relive once again some of the things you had hoped would remain hidden from view for the rest of your life. Congratulate yourself for your courage. You deserve it. Go ahead—jump in and start swimming. The results will amaze you. Believe me.

CHAPTER TWELVE

THE LOVE
OF YOUR LIFE

As we continue across the gray-green, sea-like expanse of our lives, following various arcs from marker to marker, circumnavigating our own personal globe from birth to death, we come to one particular buoy which seems a bit larger than the others. As we glide closer, we may notice a warm light emanating from it, leading upward and disappearing into the clouds above. Below, in the emerald water, the same light emanates from the bottom of the buoy, penetrating downward as far as we can see. It is a light that illuminates many events we have experienced, and bathes the face and figure of the person who has been the "significant other" in our life, the person destined to be the love of our life.

As we gaze at this light, we see that it starts at a certain place. If we study that place we see that it is, in fact, the place and time where we first met this beloved person. Now is the time for us to describe our meeting with this one who has continued to illuminate our life ever since.

This may sound rather romantic to some of you, even mystical, perhaps even quite unrealistic if your marriage(s) or relationships have not been happy. But this is the time to put aside old and new wounds, a time to return to that point in life where the white light of love was clear, where hope, beauty and awe were evident, and a path into the future began to open up.

If that path ultimately became too steep to continue, strewn with boulders too large to climb over, too misty to follow or even too straight and narrow for comfort, these difficulties need not obscure the brilliance of the light or the special qualities in your beloved which the light of love first illuminated.

The story below describes the writer's coming of age and first meeting her future mate during the late years of the Second World War.

MAN HUNT
by Betty Springer

If I had been accused of going on a "man hunt" that summer, I would have denied it vigorously. Dating had been exciting in college. There were more men than women at Iowa State College, so we Home Ec majors always had full weekends. It was exciting—maybe more so because we were so carefully supervised. Our "dates" were only allowed to come into the dorm "parlor." Almost none of the fellows had cars, so the "necking" was confined to the dark shadows of the campanile or the long goodnight kisses on the dorm steps.

With those campus romances still fresh in my mind, I graduated and took a teaching job in a small, western Iowa town. The attack on Pearl Harbor in 1941 during my junior year had seemed very distant and unreal. My younger brother was in the Navy, but it seemed more like another game. When I reached Manila, Iowa, to start teaching, I began to understand the old song, "They're either too young or too old." The 4-F's who were still in town were pretty sad, and the high school boys began to look good. The boys from the football team used to hang out in my Home Ec classroom after school. They liked checking out cooking samples, and I liked the male companionship.

After a year in Manila, I was ready for adventure. My college friend Mary Lou wrote that she wanted to vacation on the east coast. We had quite a few friends scattered up and down New England, so we could visit and see the territory. We planned our trip, going by train and making lots of stops to work and cover expenses. Mary Lou didn't tell me till later that she wanted to make the first stop in Virginia because her college boyfriend, "Rosie," was stationed there. He was due to ship out shortly, so it would only be for a short time. She went ahead and I was to meet her in Virginia.

The trip across the country was like escaping from a cloister. After a year in Manila and no men around, I was surrounded by servicemen. They were eager to get acquainted quickly and tried to make the most of the time in transit. I checked out as many as possible since I was a very patriotic girl. After all, despite my four years in college, I knew that the only real measure of a girl's success was the man she was to marry. My parents thought education was important, even for girls, but it was more of an insurance—in case I couldn't get a man who would provide for me properly.

Ft. Monroe, Virginia, turned out to be a fertile hunting ground. Mary Lou and I got jobs working in a dress shop. Men were everywhere! If I walked on the street or got on a bus, I was besieged with eager suitors. It was intoxicating after a year as a small-town schoolteacher.

Mary Lou's love finally shipped out and after a month in Virginia we headed north. We stayed with Kate, a hometown friend of mine, in Washington, D.C., for a few days. There, the dating odds were reversed. We were shocked to see Kate and her roommates brazenly trying to pick up the guys in the bars: there were so many girls working in D.C. that they became the aggressors. From there we made stops in New Jersey and New York, and then went on to Boston. I liked it there and was all set to get a job for a while. But—Mary Lou had to go to Rhode Island. Instead of being shipped to faraway places, Rosie had been sent to a Coast Artillery post in Jamestown. She *had* to go there for one more last time together, and I *had* to go with her.

In Jamestown, a resort town with some old hotels where the wealthy families from New England came for a "simple" vacation, we applied for jobs as waitresses in the hotel, were assigned a room in a nearby house as part of the pay, and arranged to meet Rosie—all in a day! Rosie looked much more exciting in uniform than he had on campus, where he was a dairy major. Being a smart fellow, he brought a blind date for me.

The blind date was another lieutenant, tall, good-looking and from Brooklyn! He was charming and full of Irish blarney. I proceeded to tell him how deprived he was to have grown up in Brooklyn. I also insisted on walking and walking—I wanted to see the area. He complained of his painful feet constantly and wanted to sit down. He had new shoes which he had worn all day, and his feet were in pain. But I had completed my basic training in coping with lonesome servicemen and was very suspicious of his motives. It's surprising that he came back after that first night.

But he did come back, every hour he could get off the post, and the weeks were measured by our time together. He was handsome, with bright blue eyes and sandy hair that had a little curl. In addition to being from New York he had traveled a lot—with the Marines to Guam and China, and with a construction crew to Trinidad. He was so sophisticated and worldly that I couldn't believe he was in love with me. There was only one barrier. He was a Catholic, and my Methodist upbringing made that a high wall. Mary Lou flatly informed me I couldn't marry a Catholic. But we were madly in love and knew that somehow we'd work that out. It all happened quickly, after the slower pace of Iowa living, but life was lived on the edge in those days. With the war, we didn't know what the future would bring.

We had a glorious few weeks and then he was shipped to another location and I had to go back to teaching. We met for a couple of days in New York before I left for Iowa. I met his father and visited at his brother's apartment. I was terrified! His father seemed stern and forbidding. The blue eyes and blarney were the gift of his Irish mother, who had died when he was six. His brother and wife were more friendly, but they came from another world. They were so different from my family.

He followed me to Iowa to meet my family and then I took off for my new job on the west coast, in Washington. We agreed we would be married, but it was hard to know when.

One morning late in November I was called to the school office to take a phone call. It was just before the start of the school day, with teachers and students coming and going in this one big office. In all this noise, my love was calling to say that he was shipping out soon and could have a furlough before he left. The big question was—"Do you want to get married, right now, before I go?" My mind was in as much of a turmoil as the noisy office. How can you murmur words of love with the whole world listening? Of course I wanted to marry, but now—without my family—so quickly? But of course the answer was "Yes!"

And so, the "man hunt" was successful. The mission was accomplished. How was I to know that was only the beginning of the story?

◊ ◊ ◊

Now find yourself that most comfortable of places, perhaps get out that photo album, put on the record player one of your favorite "oldies," and recreate that first meeting. Now write it.

◊ ◊ ◊

Once you have written about your first meeting, you may wish to continue with other stories and incidents which tell of the ups and downs of your relationship with this very special person.

If the relationship ultimately came to an end, through divorce or death, you may wish to link the various episodes together so that the character and qualities which made this person so fascinating to you are traced from the beginning to the end of your relationship. You may even show how these same qualities may have been responsible for its termination.

If you have had several marriages or relationships, each important relationship deserves to be treated in a new story, as if you two were meeting for the first time.

In the episode on trauma we dealt with the need for honest observation, and the same is true for stories of life with your beloved. No matter how the story ends, the stresses and strains of a continuing relationship deserve an honest and penetrating portrayal.

Viewing your relationships from the perspective of your first meetings may help you to recapture the bright light of idealized love as you first experienced it. You may find you have reached a fuller, deeper level of feeling, or you may have reached a place of boredom and stagnation. Perhaps the retelling may open some possibilities for a better relationship. Perhaps you have reached a point of agonizing and bitter cynicism about the future of this relationship and all others. Whatever your situation, it deserves to be recorded unclouded by your earlier feelings about that person. Each phase of life deserves to be seen accurately for what was or is there at a certain time.

If you are ready, go ahead and write about those other significant moments in this relationship. Be honest, fair and open. That is all you, your audience, or your loved ones can ask of you. "He" or "she" would want you to open up. No loyalties are being violated; most of the people who will read or hear what you are composing have had similar experiences. Sharing those experiences will help others release, relieve, and unburden themselves.

So go ahead. You are starting at the source of the shaft of light. You have done a good job of telling the story of your first meeting. If the path looks rocky, so be it; describe that rocky path. We will all profit from it. Get comfortable, and go on.

CHAPTER THIRTEEN

KIDS, KIDS, KIDS— AND PARENTS TOO

AS WE REVIEW OURSELVES CHARTING FIRST ONE course and then another across the sometimes calm, sometimes turbulent sea of life, past the shadowy markers of tragedy and trauma, past the emerald-green, light-pierced waters of love, we come to an un-usual marker. It has a bell which echoes, and in some cases there are several other, similar markers around it. Each echo has its own sound, yet also resonates with the sounds of the other bells. As we come closer we see these marker buoys have the faces of our children on them.

It is time for us to review our lives with our off-spring. Begin by listening to and savoring the sounds of that word, off-spring. Spring, as in a source of fresh water or a leap from one place to another.

There are two things to consider when listening to the echoes of our children's voices. First, we will want to recollect the significant moments in our children's lives and the feelings we experienced then. Our children, in all likelihood, will have different feelings and recollections, and they may even wish to record their own versions of the events. The second thing we may wish to do is describe the way in which we, as parents, related to our children and grandchildren—what we hoped to accomplish and what we did accomplish in having and raising our offspring. We may also wish to talk about the character and qualities we see in our children and grandchildren, and relate these qualities to those of their parents and grandparents.

This is important because at one time or another in our lives we are searching for our identity. To find certain traits in ourselves and see how they relate to our ancestors can be quite helpful. One suggestion: it may be best, when describing one's children's fundamental qualities, to use positive terms which could help to inspire them in that direction. The intertwined lives of children and parents are filled with comical, touching, powerful moments. After describing some of these, you may wish to go deeper, to reflect upon moments when your relationship changed, for better or worse. Maybe you as a parent made a decision that had a significant positive certain result, or failed to make an important sacrifice at an equally critical moment. Either event may have had a significant impact on your relationship. If you were responsible for a failure, now is the time to own up to it. Your children may not have forgiven you, but forgiveness may be closer than you think.

Or your children may have done something which hurt you, and now is a good time to get it out in the open. Not as a complaint, but as an honest story.

Resist the urge to air all your dirty laundry, though. Your remembrances will be served best by recollecting those experiences of affection, fun, sharing and exploration of the newness of life which happen in a special way between parent and child. Tessie Ross' story below is a fine example of how to describe a stressful experience without rancour, even showing it's positive effect.

OUT OF THE MOUTHS OF BABES
by Tessie Ross

The year was 1967. Carl, our son, was 9 years old and we were finally able to take a long trip that summer.

For the past few years we had been staying pretty close to home because Henry, my husband, had suffered a herniated disk at work. There had been doctor's visits, tests, painful suffering, physical therapy, and disputes with Workman's Comp. The pain finally became bearable, and we were free to live our lives again.

Carl had been sent to Camp Ramah in Ojai for the past three summers, being an only child and needing to learn to mingle, but he refused to go again, claiming we were only trying to get rid of him. I thought at that time, "Get rid of him? Just send me away there for six weeks and I would consider it heaven!" All in all, it was time for the three of us to have a vacation together, and we settled on the World's Fair in Montreal.

The travel agent's arrangements found us stuck out in the boonies in an area called Lachine. The first morning we awoke raring to go, but after the bus ride to the Metro, the Metro into town and a train out to the Fair, we were tired. It took a while to get oriented and by that time Carl announced he was hungry. It was about two o'clock so we decided to go get lunch.

Asking for the location of the restaurant area, we were directed through a very long, wide, hangar-like structure, filled with crowds rushing along as if they had a deadline to meet. There were display booths on either side of the building, and people were handing out leaflets and samples.

We were each loaded down with a jacket, Expo tote bag, camera and, of course, I carried a purse. Henry, who always walked as if being chased by the devil, soon was far enough ahead of us so we could barely see him. I had hold of Carl's hand to keep us from being separated, and though we hurried, we could never hope to catch up to Henry.

As we were going along, a young girl was handing out samples of candy. They looked like sour balls, but were about three times as large. Carl pulled me over and we both took a sample, which he promptly popped into his mouth. I knew he was hungry, so although I told him to save it I didn't say anything more, figuring it would appease his appetite until we got some food.

As we were rushing along, being buffeted by the crowds, I felt my skirt being tugged and looked down to see why. There stood my little boy with his eyes wide open and bulging, his mouth gaping and his right hand beating his cheek near his throat.

I looked at him and thought, "God! What happened?" Inside me I felt panic well up. I thought, "Here I am, alone with my kid who is choking, what am I going to do?" I started to scream, "Henry, Henry," all the while knowing that in that pandemonium no one could hear me. Then through all those waves of panic and fear came a calm voice that said, "Stop being a hysterical yenta; this is not the time for that."

Without thinking or knowing how or why I could move and make decisions, I dropped everything, knelt down, lifted Carl up, turned him upside down and started thumping his back.

While doing this a hysterical voice in my mind

was raging, "You are losing him, your sweet little boy, you dope. Why did you let him take that candy? What will Henry say? To Hell with him, he isn't even here to help."

Then I heard a gasp and saw the candy roll off down the hall. The sane, sensible part of my mind that had come to the rescue had me turn Carl right side up and set him on his feet.

Suddenly I felt all my strength go from me and I sank to my knees and grabbed Carl into a very tight hug. He threw his arms around my neck and held on for a while, gasping for breath.

I patted his face, wiped his tears, assured him he was going to be alright now. I was there and would take care of him. I told him I loved him and wouldn't allow anything to happen to him. I also said how sorry I was that I hadn't thought ahead to see that the candy might choke him.

In the meantime, my hysterical voice inside was still raging at me, telling me I was an idiot for putting Carl in such danger.

I thought my exterior was cool, efficient, comforting and loving, but when Carl let go and stood back he looked at me and in a sad voice said, "Mommy, don't cry, I'm sorry, I didn't mean to frighten you. You better get up because you are going to be thrown over; we are in the way."

I looked around and realized the people were still rushing through the structure, but somehow they had parted and gone around us, making a little island of space where we were. No one had stopped to see what was happening or offer help, but then it had all happened so fast I guess all they saw was a woman and child hugging each other.

Miraculously, our belongings had not been kicked aside, so we gathered them up and, holding each other tightly, went out to find Henry. We saw him standing at the end of the long building, peering in with an impatient look, folded arms and tapping foot. As we came close, he called out, "What happened to you, what did you stop to look at? I thought you were in such a hurry to get food. You're always dragging behind."

I was still too distraught and shaken from the experience to think logically, so I was slow in answering. It was a good thing, because the tirade I would have poured out would have ruined the vacation.

However, Carl, with no malice or anger, in a very matter of fact voice, said, "Dad, why weren't you with us? I almost choked to death. It's a good thing Mom was there to help me."

I don't know if all of what Carl said sank in, but the words, "You weren't there," hit home. Henry's face changed from annoyance and impatience to a sheepish look of guilt and, though I can't say why, fear.

But then he turned to me and, as if to divorce his feelings, said, "Why weren't you watching him; how could you let him get into such a situation?"

I was about to tell him exactly how, in no uncertain terms, when Carl said, "But Dad, why weren't you there?"

Henry knelt, put his arms about his son and said, "Cookie, you know I love you and I do care. I was there when those kids tried to beat you up on the school yard. I chased them away even if it made my heart hurt."

Carl answered, "Yes, Dad, you did, and you take care of me, but you were running way ahead of us. We were alone."

Carl did not know it, but he had touched a very sore spot remaining from Henry's childhood. At any rate, on that vacation, Henry was always at our side.

◇ ◇ ◇

One caution: there is a special trap in describing one's children. It is called sentimentality, which is waxing ecstatic about how wonderful they are long before the reader or listener has a chance to know them as people. It is better to be as objective as possible, letting different situations and the way the children dealt with them delineate their character. Then it is appropriate to write about how you felt, after the event. Of course, if the event is one in which your feelings changed progressively, from concern to fear to terror, or from amusement to laughter to hysteria, then it is appropriate to write about how you felt as the event was unfolding.

There is one question you should ask yourself before you undertake to write about your children, otherwise you will certainly confront it after you start: Are you ready to write about them? Give the question some thought. When the issue of writing about children was raised in our life-story writing classes, we found that many people were reluctant to express their feelings about them, primarily, they said, because the separation which inevitably occurs between parents and children requires rebonding as part of the healing process, and for many parents that rebonding had not yet occurred. Many were engaged in writing, not about their children, but about their parents, and this, too, was part of the process: to be able to clear the air with your children, you need to have cleared the air with your parents. So, if you have not already done so, take this opportunity to address Mom and Dad once and for all.

A loving and moving example of this is Louis Doshay's letter, "Mom" (page 195). For an honest portrayal of a difficult relationship see Gina Wilcox's story "Wrongs My Mother Brought Me" (page 191).

◊ ◊ ◊

Now sit back in your easy chair, and go back to where the stories of your children all began, perhaps where conception actually took place.

Chapter Fourteen

Other Stories

AND NOW WE BEGIN TO SEE THAT THE END OF our voyage—a return to the present—is not far away.

Before we reach land, however, we notice a group of small islands close by. We change tack and sail past these: other significant experiences we have had during our mature years—trips we have taken, memorable people we have met, successes and failures, and events that we may even have helped shape and change.

PARADOX

One possible, frequently interesting approach to these stories is to write about the presence of unpredictability, paradox and the unusual in these experiences. Most of us have, at one time or another, had a sense that life is or was playing a trick on us. Just as we were sure things were going to happen a certain way, they happened in exactly the opposite way.

The part played in our lives by unpredictability, paradox and coincidence has been recognized in all cultures. In Greece and Rome, Proteus and Mercury were mythical figures of change and uncertainty; in primitive, Native American and Meso-American cultures, "trickster" figures were and remain ever-active in the mythologies. In Christianity the devil is often seen as having some trickster qualities, as we can see in the phrase, "The devil made me do it." During the Renaissance in Italy, the goddess Fortuna was recognized as embodying the paradoxical fates which may befall one at any time.

"Tricky," unpredictable qualities may also exist in ourselves, and may come out at unusual times, leading to fun, frustration, bewilderment or defeat. So, you might try writing stories which reveal contradictions, paradoxes and ironies in you and your life—unexplained and unpredictable actions and occurrences which ultimately give rise to a fascination with how varied, mysterious and even magical life can be.

◊ ◊ ◊

Perhaps you would like to reflect upon some of your own experiences and write them down before we turn landward once more.

FAMILY HISTORY

If there are other stories concerning your family's past which you would like to write, go ahead and add these stories now. They allow those who come after you to make connections with *their* pasts. Let the reader know how you learned about the story—were you sitting on grandma's knee? taking a walk with grandpa? Tell the reader what you remember grandma or grandpa doing or feeling while she or he told you the story. That way we get the story and your relationship to the storyteller; we believe it and feel it more fully. Read Lucy MacDougall's story, "Family History (3)" (page 143) for a good example of this kind of writing. Notice the way the "frame" she creates helps us see and feel the mother's struggle to get the facts straight, and how we feel Lucy's patient yet amused concern for her mother.

A word of caution about stories of this kind: There is a temptation to be very factual, to give all the names, dates and times of events and experiences gone by. This can become boring for readers and listeners alike. What works are short, vivid descriptions of things seen, people met, and deeply experienced personal feelings.

Chapter Fifteen

Our Present
Condition And The
Voyage To The Other Side

FLOATING GENTLY TOWARD OUR SAFE HARBOR, relaxed and somewhat detached, we take a good look at our present, where we are now. We ask ourselves if we are content with the life we have lived. What must we do to accept those parts of our lives that still make us uncomfortable? How has life changed for us, inwardly and outwardly, over the years? For some of us life, outwardly, may have changed a great deal, and it is valuable to see how our inner self has responded to those changes. At this point you might like to read one such comparison. Please turn to Selma Lewin's "You Can't Always Go Home Again" (page 206). There is no final, glorious landing with trumpets playing and bands marching, not on this voyage. Nor is it like Columbus opening up a route to a new continent, where millions will follow in times to come. It is our own personal, soulful voyage, expressed in our own personal terms.

But, as with any voyage, there is excitement. As we re-experience our life's journey, we begin to realize that each tack we have taken had a reason behind it, a logic of some kind, perhaps not apparent at the time. Revisiting the past, we see that there were people with whom we would like to be reunited. Our journey may help us to do this. For some of us there is the welcome realization that our later years can be very exciting. Though the body may slow and some memory functions, overloaded with stored material, act a bit erratic, that's okay; it's our renewed relationship with our deepest past that can replenish us at this point.

In a sense it becomes a preparation for another, final voyage, the one beyond the little island of our present condition. If we are shut off from our past and present, with few friends and relatives around us, then the final voyage will threaten us as terrifying and lonely, a mirror of our present condition. Or it may offer us an escape, a desperate retreat into the unknown, as if anything might be better than the present. For those who are sick and disabled this may, in fact, seem to be a very positive alternative.

Yet, if we have prepared ourselves properly, if our love relations are intact, our dependents freed, the painful and unfulfilled parts of ourselves accepted, our life's experiences understood, accepted and passed on to generations to come, then our present condition can be a positive experience and the final voyage can be its ultimate peak.

From the reports of people who "died" and then actually returned to life—revived drowning victims, recovered surgery patients, and the like—we sense more and more clearly the existence of a life beyond our material one. As we develop a better understanding of the zone between the two worlds, we need to think about how we will prepare for whatever is "out there."

Turn now to the last story in the book, a provocative, poetic narrative by E.S. called "First Days." In the story he asks us to look at the other side of the coin, to climb into the coffin with an all-too-recently departed loved one and to share his journey beyond. What we see is this: the past and the dead have an enormous grip on the present and on the living. E's character, outward bound on the final voyage, asks the living to let go of those who have ceased to live in earth-time so they may pursue their final journey into eternal time.

CHAPTER SIXTEEN

ORAL HISTORY

OUR EFFORTS UP TO NOW HAVE BEEN DIRECTED toward creating writers where none existed before. Many people, however, for a variety of reasons, do not want to write their life stories, yet they are interested in having their histories recorded. This is certainly possible, although the techniques of writing these differ from those we have used and discussed.

These life histories, often recorded on video or audio tape and later transcribed onto paper, are known as oral histories. Sometimes the oral histories are done by the subjects themselves; at other times they are done by interviewers taping family members, friends or clients.

Whether you interview yourself or someone else, the series of questions given below will enable the persons being interviewed to reveal as much interesting information about themselves and their experiences as possible. The questionnaire is followed by a sample oral history by Nat Leventhal. Initially, Nat told his story into a tape recorder. It was then typed out, edited and retyped in the form of a story.

A second kind of oral history is the story, "Pool Hall" by Grace Holcomb. She began by recording her ex-husband's life on tape; then, using the techniques described in Part I, transformed his narrative into intense life stories using dialogue, narration, inner monologues, etc. After writing each story creatively, she checked back with him to be sure that what she had written was as close to what had happened as possible.

INTERVIEW QUESTIONS

1. What is your earliest memory?

2. What is your earliest truly strong and powerful memory?

3. Can you describe your parents, or the person(s) who raised you?

4. What were the strongest good and bad traits of your parents?

5. Do you remember any stories that illustrate these traits?

6. What is the happiest early memory you have?

7. What is the saddest or most frightening early memory you have?

8. What are some of the experiences you remember most vividly from your childhood?

9. Do you remember any friends who were particularly important to you?

10. Do you remember any interesting stories about these friends?

11. What was school like?

12. Do you remember any interesting stories about your schooling?

13. Who was the first boy (or girl) you fell in love with? What was that like?

14. Do you remember any difficult or important decisions you had to make during your early years?

15. What were some of the jobs or occupations you worked at during your life?

16. Do you remember any interesting or funny stories about your work?

17. Many times in life we remember things one way but our friends and relatives remember them differently. Do you have any experiences like this?

18. Often in life we have stories of sadness and trauma which are important to talk about. What has happened in your life that you remember with real sadness?

19. Most of us have had one person in our lives who was very important to us, a man or woman whom we have loved a great deal. Who was that person in your life?

20. What was it about that person that made him or her so special?

21. How did you meet? What were the circumstances?

22. Were there other people—teachers, counselors, friends—who helped shape your life and attitudes?

23. Who were they? What were they like?

24. Many of us have children who have given us a great deal of pleasure and pain. Would you like to describe yours?

25. Do you remember any stories that really tell something about your relationship with your children?

26. If there were one thing you would like to tell your children and those who will come after them, what would it be?

SAMPLE ORAL HISTORIES

BECOMING AN AMERICAN
by Nat Leventhal

In July of 1914, I came to the harbor of Boston. Everything looked so different to me. The people who were working at the docks had hard straw hats and they spoke a language which I couldn't understand; it was strange to me. They didn't have quotas. They just looked at you and saw if you were healthy, then they put you on a train and sent you where you belonged. Those who had to go to Boston were sent to Boston. There was not much of any kind of difference. I do not know how it was in Ellis Island, but in Boston it was not a problem.

At that time the immigrants were accepted with open arms, regardless of race, color, or whatever. Five doctors looked me over to make sure I was healthy and then I was put on a train to Chicago. My sister lived in America, and she had bought my tickets ahead of time and made the arrangements with the agent. When we got to Chicago she was waiting outside the station. There were no guards and we walked among the Americans. She recognized me and took me to her home on a streetcar.

In those years when I came, my sister had a grocery store in the front and the living quarters in the back. She had a big galley stove that used to keep us warm. We used to put coal in it and would stay around the stove. We didn't have bathtubs in the house; we went to the steam houses. We did not have toilets in the apartment. They were in the hallway and everybody got a key for the toilets. That was the life in those days, in 1914 and 1915. At that time, I used to get up about 3:30 in the morning and go with my brother-in-law to get produce for the store. We used to buy onions, potatoes, tomatoes or whatever there was. Before the farmers opened up baggage, we used to get a good buy. Then I used to sit on the wagon and my brother-in-law would yell, "Onions, dry onions, ten cents a peck!" A peck was fifteen pounds. Tomatoes were ten cents for ten pounds and potatoes were ten cents for fifteen pounds.

Then, he used to take me to buy groceries. When I was with him an incident happened. It was at South Water Street, on the waterfront. Con Edison was having an excursion. There were many people, I think about a few thousand, and a big boat, the Eastline. The people were in a gay mood. The boat was loading fast. Finally, when the people were all on the boat, they let the ropes go and the boat turned with the bottom up into the river. Thousands of people were floating in the Chicago River, and people were throwing those crates that they have chickens in, into the water. People were jumping into the water to rescue people and the whole day they were cutting the bottom of the boat to take out the people. Then the big trucks came and they took out the dead people. Those were the things I saw in my young days.

In those days when you came to a place on the Loop between downtown and home you used to get a big stein of beer for five cents, then all the smorgasbord you could eat for free. That was those days! When I stayed with my sister, I used to get a nickel and we'd get pails made out of metal which would take about fifteen glasses of beer. We used to go to the brewery and pick up a pail of this beer on hot days in the summer. The whole family used to drink beer and that was our enjoyment. When we had time on Sunday, we used to go to a park near the lake. My sister would bring sandwiches and we used to have a good time. We also had in Chicago the Jewish theater, the Jewish papers. We didn't have to use the English language so much. Most of us used the Jewish language at home, therefore we still retained our accent. We hadn't developed a real American accent.

Afterwards, I was trained to be a tailor. I first started to train when I was six years old in Russia. In America I didn't know the language, but I read the Jewish papers and found an ad for a man that knows tailoring. So, I came to work early in the morning, at seven o'clock. I did my work and at seven in the evening, I said, "I'm going home."

"What's the matter with you, half a day?" Seven to seven is half a day! So, I didn't want to work there any more.

So I went to work in a wholesale grocery. In those days, vinegar was not in bottles. It was in 57-gallon barrels. There were barrels of herring. I used to carry 100-pound bags of sugar and stack them up to the ceiling. The ceiling was about 50 feet high. Flour and salt were in 150-pound sacks. I also went on the wagon to deliver.

I was not then Americanized. In those years they

used to tell you, "Take these barrels and put them in the other room, and put something else here." Those 57-gallon barrels were impossible to handle. I didn't know how to handle those big barrels. A truck driver came over to me and said, "Young man, listen to me. Put your heels in the ground, reach up, push the barrel, and pull it back to you. Then you roll it on the floor. That's the way—just push it down and pull it up." I became an expert! I used to do this kind of work and work on the wagon with the driver like a strongman.

Then I again went to work as a tailor. In those days they used to work 56 hours a week—that was union. Pay was six dollars for the week. After six was overtime; I used to get paid extra for that. Saturday was a half day. We'd leave the job about 9:30 in the evening. So I didn't have time to go to night school. I wanted to learn, so I got a teacher that taught me how to write and read English and I became Americanized.

In those years I paid $2.50 for room and board for a week. I used to sleep on a cot. I used to eat breakfast with the Mrs. and she used to give me a sandwich to take to work. In the evenings I would come and have supper, all for $2.50.

One time I went to Mexel Street. This was like Orchard Street in New York. People had pushcarts where they used to sell things. In Europe we didn't see this. There the women came and when they were sitting in the market, they had these pots of coal under their skirt and this would warm them up. The Jews, when they came from New York, were all concentrated into one section around Roosevelt Road and 12th Street and Hostess Street. There was the Jewish theater and the Jewish newspaper and the Jewish life, like in Europe.

I went to Mexel Street to buy a pair of shoes. I

asked for a pair of shoes. I tried them on my right foot and they fit me very well. So I paid him whatever he asked and I went home. When I got home, I found out that both shoes were for one foot. So I came back and told him, "I can't wear two shoes on one foot." He grabbed me by my behind and threw me out of the store. That was the end of my shoe buying.

At that time there were no automobiles but mostly horses and wagons. I used to try to learn to jump on the streetcar, to jump on and off. That was a trick that all the youngsters used to do. I did, too. But one time I got dressed to visit my sister about fifty miles away. I jumped off one street car to take the other, and jumped wrong. I jumped straight and fell in the mud. I was all covered with mud, and when I went to my sister, she didn't know who it was. Finally she recognized me! I had to change from head to foot because I was all smeared up.

◊ ◊ ◊

POOL HALL
by Grace S. Holcomb

Our town, Collbran, Colorado, only had about 300 or so people in the 1930s while I was growing up and we had the usual assortment of stores in town.

First and foremost for adults was the Post Office. That was the general meeting place. People came in and out of there all day long, not really looking for much mail, but to pass the time of day with their neighbors.

We had a drug store, a grocery store and a barbershop with two barbers. Of course, there wasn't enough work for two barbers, so one doubled as the town's undertaker and the other was a part-time farmhand and musician at dances.

We even had a restaurant but we didn't call it that. The sign said "Collbran Cafe, Good Eats." It was just the café to us and it was where we kids would get a soda pop or ice cream if we had a nickel.

Of course Doc Ziggle had an office in town and a small six-bed hospital, and there was a small bank. We didn't have a dentist; if a tooth needed pulling, the blacksmith did it. Occasionally, if it was impacted, he would send the patient to Grand Junction.

But, by and large, the very best place in town to kids was the one and only pool hall. We loved it. As pool halls go, it wasn't much. Just a large room, with a couple of big windows, usually dirty, and an inside toilet, one of the few we had. There was a bar all along one side of the room and beer and whiskey were sold, but not too much whiskey. Mostly everybody was a beer drinker. But, if you wanted to just nurse a bottle of whiskey in private there were five or six tables and chairs. Men would just sit with the whiskey and a shot glass; they always drank it neat, and everybody knew enough to leave them alone. If they wanted company, they would sit at the bar. The tables were mostly used for playing cards. The men played pinochle and pitch during the day and poker at night.

There were three pool tables, and a billiard table. To eight- to ten-year-old boys it was great. It smelled of beer, cigarettes and pipe smoke, sweat and leather.

The owner, and sole worker, was Rosie. He was built a lot like the rest of the men, muscled and short. He had a completely bald head and just tufts of hair behind his ears which invariably held a pencil. If he wasn't busy he would let us in to play pool but not until we got pretty good at pool would he let us near the billiard table.

He'd say, "One of you kids touch that billiard table and I'll break both your legs and send you home to your M-a-a-ma." He would drag out the Mama and then chuckle, rub his head, and, wiping his hands on the front of his beer-stained apron, march back behind the bar. We would plead with him. "Ah Rosie, I'm good enough at pool, I won't hurt your table none," Wendell said. "You ain't good enough till I say you are," Rosie answered, "and until I do, keep your grubby hands off the billiard table," he added.

After about four or five games of pool Rosie would say, "Get out of here, you low-lifers, you've had enough fun for one day." We'd all scatter; we liked Rosie a lot and the pool hall too. We didn't want him mad at us.

But Rosie's pool hall also meant cowboys, for that was where they headed when they got paid and were in town to tie one on. Those poor bastards worked like dogs and pretty much lived like dogs too. They only got to town once a month when they got paid.

We were all sitting out on the porch in the front of the house when Ernest Turner came racing up yelling for me. "Ted," he yelled, "cowboys are in town." I just about jumped out of my skin because I knew what that meant. I looked at Poppa with the most pleading look I could muster and said, "The chores are all done." Poppa said, "Go ahead, have yourself a good time." He didn't even get to finish his sentence and Ernest and I were racing away.

We ran to the homes of a couple of other boys in town and then the group of us headed for Rosie's. Sure enough, when we got in there were two cowboys sitting at the bar. We ran up and asked, "Got anything needin' doing?" Sometimes we would curry their horses, or just walk and water them. But just as often they would say, "Well, I don't guess so." But they would always give us something, a penny, nickel or dime. Away we would go to the "Collbran Cafe, Good Eats" for a treat. It was about the only time we ever got soda pop or ice cream.

But today was extra special because our favorite cowboy, Walt, was there. He was always good for a dime at least and sometimes a whole quarter. We thought he was the richest man after the town's banker.

Walt liked to have fun with his money. He would boom out with his loud voice, "Here you ragtag scamps, go buy yourselves a barrel of whiskey." If Walt got too drunk we would know it and ease him off the stool so he wouldn't fall, and lay him on the floor. He'd sleep off his drunk and just lie there on the floor. Everybody would step over him and nobody paid any attention. We did our best to take care of him. He was special.

One day we heard that Walt was pretty sick and as Poppa and I were in town I asked Poppa, "Can I go see Doc Ziggle to see how Walt is doing?" Poppa said, "Sure, go ahead, but don't take all day. We got chores to do at home." Then he chuckled to himself and said, "If I was you, I wouldn't worry too much. Walt is too tough to die."

I knew Poppa was probably right, but I still wanted to hear it from the Doc so I raced over to the hospital. "Doc," I said, "How is Walt?" Doc said "Tell your Poppa that Walt had gallstones but I got them all. Ole Walt is going to be all right," he added. That made me feel a whole lot better and I passed the word to the other kids.

The next time Poppa and I were in town we saw the stones. There were on display in the barbershop window in a fruit jar. The sign on the display said, "Walt's Rocks."

The pool hall meant more to us than cowboys, Walt and Rosie. Old Dewey Fitzpatrick hung around there too. He was an old man, must have been 50 or so, and he would spin stories for us.

"Dewey, please tell us again about how you lost your fingers?" we'd plead. "Well," Dewey would say, "sure you boys can take a bloody tale?" "Oh, yes, sir," we would answer. "You ain't agonna tell your mammas I done gave you bad dreams, are you?" he asked. "Oh, no, sir," we answered in chorus.

He then proceeded to tell us how he was fighting bears and this one bear was extra special mean. Dewey beat off the bear, of course, but just for damned orneriness the bear jumped up and bit off the ends of two of his fingers. He would then hold them up for us to inspect.

That old dope would go on telling stories about skinning buffalo and fighting Indians. We figured some of his stories could be true, he sure was old enough.

He just did odd jobs around town, and was the town drunk if he could afford it, but he always had time to spin a tale or two for us, and they were never quite the same except for the bear and the fingers. He never changed that story. He'd tell us about being in the middle of a buffalo herd and a whole company of Indians came at him. "But, Dewey," we would protest, "last time it was only a few Indians." "Well, hell, boys, think that only happened once? This was a different time," he said. "Shut up now, and listen or I ain't gonna tell you no more." We would all be quiet because you never knew what he was going to say each time.

One time Dewey was in the pool hall, pretty drunk, and went into the toilet. Fred Wallace wanted to go in the toilet and old Dewey wouldn't get off the pot.

Fred was the son of Bill Wallace, one of the biggest and richest ranchers around that area, and Bill Wallace was one of the meanest sons of bitches we had. He was built and looked like a pit bull and his son Fred was just like him. Fred was about twenty when he was trying to get Dewey out of the toilet and it made him madder than hell. The other men heard the commotion in the toilet, but by that time it was too late.

Dewey was dead. Fred had dragged him off, then hit him so hard Dewey's head hit on the edge of the toilet bowl, killing him instantly.

Poppa was constable at that time so he told us this story. Poppa came and told Fred to go on home—he would decide what was to be done later.

We had no courthouse or judge in Collbran so Poppa and Fred drove into Grand Junction. Bill, Fred's father, was already in Grand Junction. Poppa came home the same day and so did Bill and Fred.

Poppa never did say what happened, and I never knew. All he would say was "Well, you know Bill Wallace has a lot of influence around here."

The town was pretty well divided over whether Fred should have gone to jail, but with time, it was forgotten. But the little boys of the town, of which I was one, never forgot it. We all wished we were bigger—we wanted to hang Fred ourselves. We all wanted to be the one to tie the noose. We missed old Dewey. He had been our friend. The pool hall was never quite the same with Dewey gone.

CHAPTER SEVENTEEN

PUTTING IT
ALL TOGETHER

HAVING FINISHED THE STORY OF YOUR LIFE, an undertaking of many months, perhaps even years, you will want to put it together or "package" it in a way that will give you a sense of accomplishment and have a pleasing effect on those who read it. You've tackled the project as seriously as any artist would, and your work deserves to be mounted properly. In the following short chapter there are some hints about "wrapping it all up": illustrating your work, presenting each page in the most readable way, using calligraphy and ornamentation to enhance the work, reproducing and binding copies handsomely, and selecting an appropriate cover for the finished book.

Just as we anticipate with pleasure what will be found inside a nicely wrapped Christmas gift or birthday present, so the little extras which we add to our finished volume will give our readers a sense of anticipation and delight when they pick up our work.

PAGE DESIGN AND LAYOUT

Your narratives are worth preserving and should be as readable as possible. Unless you have a very readable and artistic handwriting, they should be typed or printed using a word processor (or, these days, a personal computer) with a good printer. The printer should have "letter quality" type; be careful of dot matrix printers which look "computer-ish" and may not reproduce adequately. Test them first to see that they have a letter-quality mode. And look into using laser printer facilities that are now available in some copy-and-quickprint franchise shops.

If your work is typed, earlier drafts should be double-spaced, but the final version can be done with one and a half spaces. A one inch margin should be allowed on three sides of the page, with an inch and a half for the left-hand, or inside, margin, where you will bind the book. Help the reader by treating special elements of the text, like poetry or quotations, in a special or distinctive way. One common technique is to indent these sections or elements about a half inch from the left margin. Always remember to indent the beginnings of new paragraphs, though it is not necessary to leave a whole extra line between paragraphs.

If you should decide to get your book laser-printed, find someone with an understanding of book design and typography to help you design the basic page layout. And if you have the book professionally typeset, always use a *book* typesetter, not someone whose main typesetting experience is with advertising or newsletters and flyers.

ILLUSTRATIONS

"A picture is worth a thousand words" is the old cliché, and it truly will enhance your work to include photographs, drawings, even carefully chosen memorabilia pasted up in the pages of your book. If you plan to have a number of copies of your life story made, you may make photocopies of the photographs and place them in the text. For better quality at a slightly higher cost you could get duplicate photographs, or ask your local small printer to get you "photostats." Be sure to leave room in the text for the photos as you are typing it or printing it out, or ask a local graphic artist or graphic arts student to help you to "cut and paste" the final text.

A hand-made drawing is another and very delightful type of illustration. One very creative idea was suggested in a class by a student writing the life of her mother. As she finished each story, she had her young daughter illustrate it with drawings. The resulting collection of stories with illustrations was given as a present to the student's mother on her birthday, and a second installment at Christmas time. It was a deeply heartfelt experience shared by three generations of a family.

TITLES AND HEADINGS

The first page of each story should be treated a bit differently, and book designers frequently use ornamental capitals or special sizes and typefaces for chapter headings and openings. As a basic page layout, you might start the title of the story one or two inches from the top of the page, and start your first line of text about two to three inches below the title. This is a generally used, fairly standard approach, and you should feel free to make as many creative variations on it as you wish.

For examples of some of the design elements we have talked about, look again at the treatment of titles, chapter openings and page layouts in this and other books.

Another way of giving your narrative a nice look is to use calligraphy in appropriate places. Calligraphy, which is elegant, stylized handwriting done by specialists, can be used to nice effect as chapter or story headings, as in the following:

Right Your Are If You Think You Are

Calligraphy or special designs can also be used as ornamentation, to give style to the first letter of a chapter or text:

HISTORIANS of art like to present the turn of the century as an Epoch and begin a new chapter even when describing Northern painting.

The reader may think calligraphy and ornamentation are too fancy for his or her narrative, but in fact they add a personal, hand-crafted feel to a volume of stories and experiences, which is itself very personal and handcrafted. So calligraphy is entirely appropriate in such a work.

A good way to find calligraphers and obtain advice about graphic design is to consult the list of course offerings at your local adult school, community college and art school, or consult the art department of any high school or college in your area.

REPRODUCTION, COVERS AND BINDINGS

At the present time, photocopying techniques allow one to reproduce one's work fairly inexpensively. Likewise, inexpensive, attractive covers and bindings may be obtained at most printing shops for a few dollars and will add a very nice appearance to your work. The commonly available binding options are *velo binding,* where the pages of the book have holes punched in them and a black plastic strip attached on both sides that holds the book and covers together, and *comb binding,* where the pages and cover are held together by a broad comb, making it look rather like a spiral notebook. The velo binding is generally neater and has more strength; the comb binding is better for thick books and those that need to lay open easily. To see examples of these bindings go to your local copy shop, and select what looks and feels best to you.

More expensive binding options include perfect binding, where the pages are glued together inside a cover, and case or cloth binding, which is done using a hardcover case. These are generally too expensive for one, two or even fifty copies of a book, but if you are interested then look in your local yellow pages under "bookbinders" or ask at your library for the name of a library binder.

◊ ◊ ◊

Now that you have reviewed the stages of your life, you may be better able to see the directions it has taken, and how you have responded to the challenges that presented themselves at different times. Perhaps this review has enabled you to see your journey and your goal more clearly, and given you a better sense of who you are. It has probably enriched your writing as well, allowing for a deeper contact with yourself and a freer, more confident expression of your feelings.

Through writing about their life experiences, people rediscover a sense of awe about and a fascination with the unpredictability and absurdity, the joy and the mystery of the world we live in.

In Part III you will read other stories which reflect some of these qualities of life.

PART THREE

LIFE WRITING
SELECTIONS

The stories which follow are selections from works written by students in our life-writing classes in Los Angeles between 1983 and 1987. They were written using the techniques outlined in Parts I and II of this book and serve as effective examples of the methods—and rewards—of writing from within. I hope you will find them enjoyable to read, and they may stimulate in you recollections of a similar kind, recollections which you may someday want to write.

FAMILY HISTORY (3)

by Lucy MacDougall

M Y MOTHER WAS DOZING AFTER LUNCH WHEN
I got to her room in the nursing home. Three
nickels she won at Bingo were still in her lap. She woke
right up at the prospect of an Eskimo Pie and her week-
ly copy of the *National Enquirer,* which she has told me
at this point in her life she enjoys more than the Bible.

"How have you been?" I asked.

"Fine," she said. At death's door, in the grip of gray
depression or desperation, my mother always said fine.

I sat on the edge of her bed, scanning the state of
her health in the wheelchair for myself as she bit into
the chocolate covering. Would I be like that in 25 years,
with occasional spurts of spirit and energy, living days
the size and shape of postage stamps?

Her gaze, though, was intent still. She'd gobbled
the Eskimo Pie while I was staring at her. Now she was
staring at me, impatient, ready to get on with it.

I picked up my pencil and paper in a hurry.

"I was my father's favorite," she said right away.

My mother had been waiting patiently for days while I poked around in the past for her immediate ancestors. Now she was looking forward to being born and getting on with her own personal firsthand memories. Three other babies had to be born first. "Edward came first," she said, "then Albert and Percy, and I came next." Her mother named her Irene Jeannette Scherrer. 1883. The first girl.

Her face suddenly clouded. I knew. It was going to be about Percy. It was always sad about Percy. Little Percy got sick with diphtheria and my grandmother and the housekeeper took care of him, but it was while Grandma was at work that he died. "Your Grandma would never go back to work after that. She took care of us and did piecework at home. Percy was her favorite," she explained.

"But I was my father's favorite," my mother said again, anxious to make herself once more the rightful star of her own story. "Much more than Roma."

Here comes Roma, upsetting the order of the years. Here she comes, pushy pushy little sister, on the scene in my mother's memory when my mother's barely gotten herself born yet. "Just like her," my mother said when I mentioned it, the surface of her placidity shaken even after over eighty years by the appearance in the family of Roma with her dark hair, dark eyes, rosy skin, her fresh, demanding, little-girl ways, not taking any time to be a baby in my mother's memory.

"Eddie would ask her for a glass of water," my mother said, "and she'd bring it to the table and *spit* in it before she gave it to him."

"Wait a minute. That's later, when Aunt Roma's a little girl. She's not born and you're not even five yet." "I don't remember anything until then," insisted my mother stubbornly. "That's the way Roma was. But my father liked *me* more because *I* took after the Scherrers. They were very well-bred people, I told you that, and *I* took after that side of the family."

So my mother didn't want to be like her mother any more than I wanted to be like mine, or my daughters want to be like me. She had great admiration for her mother's fine qualities, but also seemed to feel a little above her. I asked her about this.

She stirred uncomfortably. It was too late in life to bother to lie. "Well, a little," she confessed.

But my mother absolutely hated Roma. Probably because she felt my Grandma spoiled Roma. "She let her get away with anything," my mother complained now for the thousandth time. Since my Grandma was a gentle, quiet person, she must have had it hard to keep Roma in line. I asked about Roma's terrible sins. My mother's anger was good as new. "My *shoes*," she cried. "I was saving them for best and when I went to wear them, she'd worn them out. And borrowing my best kid gloves from my bureau drawer, without asking, of course, and she *stretched them*." Roma's real sin, though, I can see, was taking center stage, struggling to take over princess position in the family. My mother was still freshly outraged when she thought of it.

She had told me about her life as a child so many times. To get her mind off Roma, I told her my memories of what she had told me in the past. She smiled, reliving them. The old joys softened her grievances. Wearing a mulberry satin hair ribbon on the braids of her fine hair, ruffles on the dresses her mother sewed for her, carrying her roller-skates from the hard-packed dirt of Watts Street to another Village street, Mulberry, I think, where a man with a store had put in a stretch of cement in front. Roller-skating for hours.

"I didn't go to school until I was 7. Your Grandma taught me at home," she said. When she finally went to school, they put her in third grade.

"I was very smart," she said pridefully. "My brother, Eddie, and I learned piano. The German teacher rapped our knuckles for any mistakes. Eddie would practice for hours, but the teacher said I had more talent, even though I didn't practice." Her face warmed at the thought of being able to top the brother at something.

"Talent needs practice," I pointed out, becoming the mother.

She didn't agree. "Eddie got the bicycle *just* because he was a boy. He got the camera. He went on day trips with my father. He got it all, *just* because he was a boy." She still resented it. She had to have something more and better than he did, so she'd kept the teacher's remark deep inside for years to balance the books.

She'd kept everything deep inside, that was her style. She never told Eddie or Roma or anyone in the family how she felt. "It made me sick. Roma and Eddie fighting all the time over who got what. I couldn't stand it. I'd crawl under the dining room table and hide there until it was quiet and I could come out."

"How many children did your parents have? You told me nine once, and that four survived. Is that right?"

"Did I? I don't remember that at all." My mother counted on her fingers. "Let's see, Ed and Percy and me and Roma and Harold and Albert—he died when he was a baby—and Roma and—and—nine did I say?" She shook her head. "I've forgotten. I don't know. The rest must have been babies she lost, too."

Harold was the change of life baby for my Grandma, a blue baby, my mother said. I remember Harold was always dear to her. I liked him, too. An agreeable moon-faced man when I was a little kid. He was born to my Grandma when my mother was 12. Harold Blessing Scherrer, named after some friends of Grandma's. Grandma liked to name her children after her friends to honor long associations.

"I brought him up," my mother said proudly. "I carried him around. I fed him and dressed him and changed his diapers." She'd told me that again and again, and what a help it was to Grandma, who hadn't counted on her last little Blessing.

My mother got a bit confused about this now. "I had this little son, Brian. He was my little boy."

"No, Mom," I said gently. "That is *my* son. He's your *grandson*."

"Oh. Yes. That's what I mean. It was Harold who was my son."

"No. He was *like* a son. Remember?"

She shook her head. She couldn't seem to get it right.

"You were 12 or 13 and he was your *mother's* baby. You took such good care of him," I added.

She averted her face. "Of course," she said, but I could tell she was embarrassed that she hadn't got that stuff straight.

She was tired. The past was pictures in her head and in mine, but it was more than that. The pictures filled our whole bodies, took them over. We were both tired.

That was enough for today.

SELECTION TWO

GOIN' SOUTH

by Rosalind Belcher

WHAT CAN BE MORE EXCITING THAN RIDING on a Pennsylvania railroad train and you're seven years old and it's 1946?

"You're goin' home baby. Goin' home to Georgia. Goin' home to see yo' brothers and grandma and auntie."

That's what they told me.

Feeling grown up and scared at the same time. Opening up my boxed lunch of fried chicken, bolony sandwiches made with Wonder Bread and lots of mayonnaise, just like I like it. Eatin' all my lunch up, 'cept for my plums. Savin' them for dessert.

The train is movin' fast. I'm looking out the window. All the tall buildings are gone. Now I'm watching little box-like-looking houses that stand straight in a row. All the houses have three front steps leading to the doorway. Choo-choo choo-choo...

The nice tall man in the blue suit, wearing the funny hat that has a beak like a bird, walks up the aisle. His navy blue uniform has the shiniest gold buttons I've ever seen. They almost make me blink. He carries little pillows under his arms.

"Pillow? Pillow? Hi there little missy, would you like a pillow?"

—He's talking to me. "Yes, I'd like a pillow."

"Here y'are missy; what's your name? Where ya going?"

"I'm going to Savannah," I answered, "I'm going to see my grandmother and auntie and brothers." I continued chewing the last bit of chicken in my mouth. Later, the man in the uniform smiles at me as he goes down the aisle giving the fat lady that just got on the train a little while ago a pillow. I never told him my name.

I hear him call out, "Baltimore, Baltimore!" He again moves up the aisle. He stops, not looking at me, "You, go back to that car, back there!" He never looked at me; his smile is all gone. I hate him. With my lunch box, pillow falling, even a hard boiled egg falls that I didn't know I had, I walk back. I hate him. Finally, I'm in the back of the train. All the faces back here are sad, tired, scared looking, faces of brown and black people.

Savannah, Georgia, 1946. I haven't seen my grandma or brothers or auntie since mamma and I left with my other aunt three years ago. Mamma and I live up north now with Big Auntie. It still feels funny when I call Dot "mother." One day, Big Auntie said, "Pumpkin, you should call your mother 'mother,' and not Dot." "OK," I said. I've never called her Dot since. Seems just like it was yesterday they said, "Now it's time to go home and see the family. Make things better between all of us." That's why I'm on the train goin' to Georgia.

My brothers look really funny. Big, too. They talk funny. Say things like plait when they mean braid. Tote when they mean carry. It's fun. I'm talkin' like that too, in no time. Talkin' funny, havin' a ball.

One day, Big Mamma says to Auntie, who we call

Sister, "Sister, take Pumpkin and the boys with you today when you deliver the ironin'. Stop by yer' Cousin Suzy's house so she gets a chance to see Pumpkin. Let Pumpkin show off and talk proper like." I'm feeling excited inside. I'm going to meet a new relative. Hot dog!

Me and the boys trail Sister down the dusty Georgia streets. Walkin' down West Broad Street, lookin' at the funny stores side by side; beauty parlor, barbershop, funeral parlor, market. Lookin' at the dusty boys shootin' their dusty marbles in the dusty streets while the little girls chase each other with dusty shoes and dusty legs. Some are even barefoot. West Broad Street, Georgia. Hot. Mosquitoes nipping my arms and legs before I can swat 'em away. Me and the other boys don't say much. Every now and then we steal a glance at each other. Walkin' along West Broad Street with Auntie Sister deliverin' ironin'.

The last house on the corner is Cousin Suzy's. How far have we walked? What a pretty house. Daisies on top of daisies on each side of the walkaway. Pretty white house, white shutters, pretty daisies. "Cousin Suzy," Sister calls, "Cousin Suzy, it's me, Sister and the churin." From out of the screen door comes this little round lady with this red round face and even redder cheeks. Her brown hair is almost on her shoulders. Her eyes are green and they're smiling at me. She stops and says. "Hush yo' fuss gal, I hear ya. Come on 'round the back of the house. Hello there, you must be Pumpkin," she says to me. How can this white lady be our Cousin Suzy, I wonder as a quiet hello comes out of my mouth. She gives us lemonade, and before we can finish she is sort of shooing us on our way. She gives Auntie Sister the $3.00 for the ironin' and says, "Give ya Ma my reegaards. Now you little ones better get goin' before it gets dark." It's a long time before dark.

It's nighttime now. I'm lying in my bed. The house is quiet. I've lived through another hot Georgia day. I

hear Sister crying as she talks to Big Mamma in the
room next door. She's telling Big Mamma how bad it
makes her feel every time Cousin Suzy makes her come
'round the back of the house. I hear Big Mamma say,
"Oh God, Sister, how can people be so hateful?" As I drift
off to sleep, I see my friend in his uniform on the train
giving out the pillows, then I see him makin' me go to
the back of the train, I see Cousin Suzy makin' me go to
the back of the train, I see Cousin Suzy makin' us go to
the back of the house. A tear rolls down my face and I
wonder, Is this why me and mamma left Georgia?

SELECTION THREE

LIFE ON THE RAILROAD

by Eugene Mallory

THE YEAR WAS 1904. NOT A GOOD YEAR FOR THE overbuilt midwestern railroads or the ever-distressed farmer either.

The Missouri Pacific Red Ball freight was two hours out on a night run west. The nearly new Baldwin 4-8-2, burning clean Colorado coal, was really showing what it could do.

Conductor William Sidel was riding the high seat in the cupola of the darkened caboose and pondering what he should do with his upside down life, in general. First as a boomer brakeman, so called because he and many other bold young men had followed the railroad expansion of the late 1800s wherever the new rails led. Always moving on to new runs, new towns.

Then a bit of luck, and a bit of the old blarney, and he had his own train on the Hampton, Algona and Western, riding the varnish, not a crummy caboose. Even if the varnish was only an old combination coach;

half seats, half mail and baggage, and his little conductor cubbyhole. The coach had to be there to satisfy the franchise, and he had trundled it up and down the 90 miles of lightweight rail that was all the Hampton, Algona and Western ever amounted to. No matter that many grand names had been painted over or that the old coach was hung on the end of an untidy string of freight cars and seldom exceeded 20 miles per hour, it was varnish.

A perfect old man's job, while he was still young, had perhaps made him old in too few years. God forbid!

But why was he uneasy on this perfect prairie night? True, when he had totaled his manifests, the weight of this train had shocked him, and now, his certified reliable watch said they had covered 40 miles of track in the last hour. Things had changed while he had vegetated on the "branch," as the Hampton, Algona and Western was always called. Now it was a branch. Another proud name painted over on the old coach. Just an Iowa Central Branch, and an Iowa Central oldtimer had promptly bumped William Sidel from his cushy job.

Here he was glad the office and his crew didn't know he had never been in charge of as fast and heavy a train as this was. But then, few people had. The Baldwin man in the cab proved that. He was there to see what the new high-pressure engine would do on the long slow rise from the Missouri to the high plains.

But he, William Sidel, was responsible for this monster of a train. Responsible, too, for a wife, and child to come. The easy life on the branch had led to that too. Waving to the neighborly people. Chatting with the few riders going a few miles in the old coach. Soon the school teacher stood in the window and waved with her hands behind her back so the students wouldn't see. See what that had led to. Now he was leaving her behind at nearly fifty miles per hour and lucky he was in charge and not riding the rods or cowering in an empty.

The hard times that had finished the Hampton, Algona and Western had put many hard and bitter men to riding the freights to search for that Big Rock Candy Mountain.

Not that the Hampton, Algona and Western needed much to kill it off. Probably it was never meant to survive. The Iowa Central wanted the first 70 miles as a link between its two main lines, so they put up a little real money and got Tim Branan to promote and sell stock and even put up some of his own money. Sidel thought he was pretty smart, buying five puny shares. He put up a month's pay to get a conductor's job. He thought the Central was in on the Milwaukee's refusal of a connection and even a crossover in Algona.

So, our railroad ended in an open field on the outside of Algona and no Western at all. Just a water tank, a turning Y, a primitive engine area, a tiny station, and that coal chute. The only exciting thing on the branch.

The chute was a steeply inclined trestle work, high enough that coal shoveled over the side of a car into a bin was high enough to slide into the tender. High enough, that is, if the little old engine was in the mood to push a car up there. There was enough track past the chute so that a couple of empties could be left there. Every third carload an extra trip was made to bring the empties down.

He'd never forget the day that Flanagan started up with a carload when there were three empties already up there. The only time Algona knew we were out there was when a car went up or down. You could hear that old engine snort for a mile. Not a thing could be done about it. No use to holler, just watch the empty go over the end. Flanagan got sent down for a while. The new man, off the Central board, took a look at the contraption and said, "Well, I heard he was drunk, now I know he was!" The new man took it up though. It was that or load coal into baskets and walk the ties.

"Hell of a way to run a railroad. Hell of a way for the Central to get a cheap line. Swindled the stockholders, swindled Branan, swindled me, and they'll swindle the bastards that took my job, too," mused Sidel.

Sidel came back to reality with a sudden jolt of fear. He smelled fire. A hot box at this speed could burn off an axle in a hurry and pile up hundreds of tons of splintered wood, tangled iron and smashed freight. Almost at once he realized that the fire was not a hot box, but a hobo fire in a little patch of brush in a culvert.

The shock broke the mood. Why was he woolgathering in the dark about the pokey old branch. Here he was with a fast train, a clear track, perfect weather, a harvest moon, and a million stars. How often he had longed for the excitement of the good old days. This was better, this was his train.

Sidel swung down from the dark into the cone of yellow light below the big circular tin shade of the caboose lamp. He came down lightly enough to be a young man and by first glance was astonishingly young for a conductor. A further glance showed neither a young man nor a youthful middle-aged young man, perhaps an old young man. The light brown wavy hair was just a little dulled and faded, the blue eyes too. A shrewd observer would have known the hair was thinned a bit on top beneath the striped denim cap. A face that had aged, however unwillingly, but had not achieved the solidity and maturity of early middle age. Cold comfort that might have been for the loss of the effervescence of youth and the vigor of youth and the sheer physical charm of this man. The lack of maturity and settled purpose showed plainly and not to advantage.

Jack Scott, the rear brakeman, was a startling contrast. Much the same size, build and real age, his face had long ago settled into hard, sour solidity. The face of a man who took what he could, gave only what could be required of him, and thought anyone who did otherwise was a fool. He did wonder sometimes in a dim way why he found life such a miserable affair, but not to any effect. Not a pair of men designed for easy friendship.

Jack spoke first. "What ya see up there? Are we lousy?"

"Not a soul, just a lot of moonlight."

"That fracas in the yards must have scared 'em off for a while."

Sidel did not answer. He was not pleased by this approval of "that fracas." Some hobos had shown fight. The yard dicks had used their guns, and gut-shot men had died in agony on the cinder of the yards. He had never believed the contest between the men who would ride for free and the men supposed to keep them off warranted the use of weapons as coldly lethal as a gun. A man forced off a speeding train could be killed, but he had a good chance. They could be killed trying to get on a moving train too. They knew that when they decided to get aboard. Their choice all the way.

Sidel finally spoke, "I'm going up to the head end. I'll send Fred back."

Jack answered with an edge in his voice, "Better wait a bit. The grade gets stiffer soon. That will slow her down some. It's pretty lively out there. It ain't your parlor aisle you know."

Sidel suppressed a chuckle. If Jack could see that old combination coach. However, he just said, "When we hit the grade I'm liable to get a face full of smoke and cinders. I'll go now."

He started for the door, then stopped and picked a hickory brake stick off the rack. A stick heavy enough that a man could put it through the spokes of a hand brake and put his back into it.

"You going to stop us with that?"

"We're not going to stop, but I could have some passengers who don't like the accommodations. If so, it might help persuade them to get off."

Jack's look of contempt at the weapon confirmed a building suspicion. Jack probably was carrying a gun, a derringer, no doubt. A breach of rules. Like a ship's captain, the conductor was the one authorized to carry a gun, and he was not, never had been.

He thought of bracing Jack with this charge, but decided not tonight, why spoil the run.

If that suspicious bulge was a sneak gun, and Jack had enough enemies to warrant carrying it, someone might well get on Jack's train, not looking for a ride, but looking for Jack. I'd like Jack better on somebody else's train. I'll deal with Jack later. This is my night to be the railroad man I thought I was, up there in the sloughs, he thought.

Sidel stepped out onto the front platform of the caboose. Glad to leave the unconquerable aroma of kerosene flavored with ancient tobacco and equally ancient sweat. Outside, the early fall air had nearly the sensuous, balmy feeling of the first spring thaws.

He was relieved to be free of Jack's company and potential problem, as well as the stink of the caboose. Turning, he slung the brake stick over his shoulder on its thong and mounted to the top of the train. Standing on the three-board catwalk, he paused to get the feel of the sway, wiggle and bounce of the car. The wind of passage was strong, but steady. Holding the heavy hickory in front with both hands, he took a tentative step or two and was pleased to feel the old skill coming back. Once learned, never forgotten. Now to work.

Moving steadily forward, leaning on the wind, the muscles and nerves of his legs and body checked for abnormal motion underfoot that would indicate trouble in the tracks or structure. His ears searched for the rattle, bangs and squeaks of the tail end sound. The sound that tells the dedicated train watcher that the end is coming, long before he can see the caboose. He heard no sound of dragging parts or other problems. His nose, ever alert for the acrid reek of smoldering cotton wadding and scorched grease that means a hot box, gave no bad news.

All this was largely automatic, leaving him time to be aware of the idyllic scene. The moonlight was silver, bright enough to yellow the headlight beam far ahead. The steam from the stack was heavy, lazy and rolling low, sometimes tumbling on the grass of the shadowy prairie. Not a flat plain, but a rolling country. He could smell the sweet aroma of maturing grass and the powerful, unforgettable odor of new-mown grass.

The sound of the engine became ever plainer. The clear bell-like sound confirmed the message of the cool, heavy steam. The engine was running easily on very early valve cutoff. The steam was heavy, being fully expanded in the cylinders. The heat it had picked up while hot coals had been all converted into forward motion. He had a professional appreciation of the men who had made and were operating this marvelous machine. For hundreds of centuries men had been limited to the speed and power of horses. Now the power of 2000 horses was in one machine with speed unheard of a lifetime ago.

This was railroading. This had drawn him, a teenage boy, from that long-ago and faraway place he had once called home.

His steps slowed as the realization filtered through the sensory flood that this, too, must end. He had reached a heavy-laden car of mining supplies. One that might fail under the pounding of the long fast run, but all was well. Indeed, it seemed a steadier platform than the others.

He came to a stop near the front, immersed in the intensity of experience, his eyes enamored of the kaleidoscope of grays from silver to sable in the rolling tumbling steam so close alongside, his whole being pervaded by the tremendous pulse of the engine. Rocked by the motion of the boards beneath his feet and leaning into the rush of sensuous air, he moved into an eternal moment of his own, outside the relentless pressure of events. A moment without beginning and without end, filled forever by the mighty voice from the stack, the roar of power, the power of 2000 horses.

But relentless time is not so easily stopped. A furtive figure is on the boards behind him, holding high a huge iron bolt.

The fearful blow is struck. The bony citadel of the skull is breached and the tender brain invaded. The boomer spirit flies, taking with it its eternal moment.

The useless weapons, iron and hickory alike, drop into the shadows. The dying body, in reflex of escape, stumbles forward, is supported fleetingly by the rushing air, then into the terrible mill below. A mill where a multitude of iron wheels beat and grind on steel rails.

The killer is already scrambling down the irons to the lowest stop, where he will fling himself away to roll and tumble on the grass like the steam. Unlike the steam, he will arise again, battered but triumphant, to bear away his bitter prize of vengeance.

The train steams on, proclaiming its puny power to the uncaring sky. In its wake are fragments of cloth, flesh and bone. Between the rails lies a railroad watch that will never measure time again.

This gruesome grist of that terrible mill will be duly gathered and sent to the newmade widow. She will pack the watch away in an attic box. The pitiful remnant of a man will be buried in the stranger's grave on the Ferris lot. Others will come to share that plot with him, but never his widow or his unborn son. They will have each other's lives to live, other graves to fill.

◊ ◊ ◊

Conductor Sidel was Eugene Mallory's mother's first husband. Gene often sat beside the unmarked grave wondering about the man, holding the watch given to him by his mother. Years later, as an employee at Rockwell Corp., the dimension and vision of this story appeared to him in the midst of a routine machining task. Not until he began reaching backward in his life-story writing did he realize the vision was that of Sidel's death. He then began to write it.

SELECTION FOUR

THE TYPHOON OF FORTY-FIVE

by Edward R. Boyle

FIRST DRAFT

AS A YOUNG SAILOR IN 1945, I SERVED AS A signalman aboard a patrol craft. These ships were not large. Just 125 feet long and 28 feet wide. During wartime they carried a crew of 125 men.

Our station at this time was three miles outside the harbor of Okinawa. We were on picket duty guarding against submarines and enemy aircraft.

The day the typhoon hit started just like other days at sea. The sun rose in the east, the ocean gave no indication of what we were in for.

At around eleven we received word that there was a storm. We had noticed the ocean swells were getting larger but no message was recorded in the log. The Captain radioed the watch and also doubled the lookouts for clouds and for any change that might appear in the ocean.

Most of us were young men and had been through

storms at sea before so we gave it little thought. Little did we know what was in store for us.

My regular watch this day was from 12 noon to 4 P.M. I arrived on the bridge at 11:45 A.M. The signalman on duty informed me of the orders which had been issued. I relieved him and took charge of the bridge.

Our assigned patrol area was a stretch of ocean six miles long which we just traveled back and forth.

All was serene for the first hour of my watch. Then the sea became a little more restless, the swells a little larger and we could see a few white caps. Still no clouds in the sky, however.

The Captain, sensing trouble I'm sure, ordered all watertight hatches closed. All of the equipment that might shift was securely tied down. We all got into our foul-weather gear for we knew that there was going to be some kind of trouble. All hands that were not needed had been sent below. Those who remained on deck were the Captain, the boatswain's mate, two lookouts and myself.

It wasn't long after these precautions were taken that the lookout shouted, "Rain clouds to the southwest. Ten to fifteen miles." All eyes immediately turned in that direction. From southeast to northwest and as high as we could see into the sky was the most terrifying sight I have ever seen. It was not only night descending upon us but it was fearful lightning and crashing thunder. Being pushed ahead of this was a howling wind that screeched like a herd of banshees, and rain that felt like a thousand needles that tried to drive right through you.

Within minutes our ship was engulfed in the most awe-inspiring yet terrifying spectacle I believe nature can produce. Our ship was bounced like a cork upon the water. Lightning flashed around us so close that I was sure I could reach out and touch it. Immediately after the flash the thunder was so loud it made the ship shudder. We could hear the steel in the ship strain as it was being twisted almost beyond its limits.

The initial fear did not last long. There was too much to do. The Captain was giving orders to the wheelhouse as to the course and speed we were trying to maintain. The lookouts had lashed themselves to their posts to keep from being washed overboard. The boatswain's mate and I were working the searchlights because by that time the sea had a lot of floating debris that had broken loose from moorings in the harbor.

We finally received orders to get inside of the harbor where there would be a little more protection. We were able to enter the harbor dodging all manner of floating junk.

Our main purpose now was to find something to tie up to. We finally spotted an anchor buoy. The Captain asked Boats "If I pass close enough can you jump and grab the ring?" Boats answered, without hesitation, "Yes, sir."

The boatswain hung outside the ship's rail. I held the searchlight on the anchor ring, and the two lookouts stood ready with the securing lines.

The Captain kept the ship's speed at five knots and just about scraped the anchor buoy. Boats made the nicest four point landing I'd seen in a long time and he had both hands on the ring. The ship had gone about 50 yards beyond the buoy so we had to back up to get near it again. We were all tense but were ready. As we neared the buoy the lookouts tossed their lines to Boats. After the bow and stern were secured we all heaved a sigh of relief.

The Captain ordered all four of us to his cabin. His only words were, "You men did a good job. Do you know you have been on deck for 20 hours?" Handing us each a half-pint of medical brandy he said, "Drink this and stay in your sack until you wake up and thanks fellows."

◊ ◊ ◊

As members of the class listened to the story, they wanted to know much more about this dramatic, exciting moment in Ed's life. In his rewrite below, Ed provides us with more descriptions of what happened moment to moment. He includes more dialogue, allowing us to see and feel the characters more vividly, and shares much more of his own inner thoughts. As the story builds to a climax, he gives us an increasingly vivd sense of what it was like to be there, expanding the moments of greatest tension. It is interesting that the description of his journey deep into the bowels of the ship to retrieve a flare gun, which has a definite symbolic, heroic aspect, did not appear in the first draft at all.

FINAL VERSION

As a young sailor in 1945, I served as a signalman aboard a patrol craft. They were the smallest real fighting ships in the navy. These ships were only 120 feet above the waterline. The mast rose 35 feet above the deck and the yardarms stretched out to ten feet. She carried a wartime crew of 125 men. On her bow was mounted one five-inch gun which could exchange fire with any surfaced submarine. On her main deck, fore and aft of the bridge and wheelhouse, were 20mm anti-aircraft guns, four on each side. Our stern was decorated with two twin 40mm pom-pom anti-aircraft guns. We had plenty of firepower if we got into a big scrap. The one gun we had on the flying bridge was at my battle station, a .50 caliber machine gun, jokingly called "Boyle's Pea Shooter." I only mention this gun because I was not allowed to shoot it. The captain grinned when he assigned me this station. "I want you on the bridge, Boyle, but don't fire that damn gun. You'll wipe out half our crew." I might have, too.

The smallness, speed and maneuverability of our patrol craft made her a rather hard target to hit. Our larger fighting ships often thought we were pests until we got into a scrap and started biting. Then they were glad to have us on their side.

Our assigned station was three miles outside the harbor of Okinawa, a stretch of ocean six miles long. In this stretch of ocean we patrolled back and forth, using our sonar to detect enemy submarines and our radar for spotting aircraft. Every man on deck and on the bridge was trained as a lookout no matter what his other duties were.

The day the typhoon hit was like so many other days at sea. The sun rose in the east, the sky was clear with a light breeze blowing, the ocean was like a sheet of fun-house glass. Just smooth lazy swells. At eleven in the morning we received a radio message that there were storms brewing southwest of our position. The captain ordered a close radio watch and double lookouts. He ordered them to keep an eye out for clouds and any change in the ocean that might occur.

Most of us were young men and had been through storms at sea before, so we gave it little thought. The sun was just a bright as ever and the sea had not changed since early morning. Still rolling gently were the soft swells that can lull you to sleep when at sea. The air was as fresh as an autumn day in the north woods. We could smell the faintest tinge of salt.

My regular watch was 12 noon to 4 P.M.. I arrived on the bridge at 11:45. The signal man on duty, Stew Gray, informed me of the radio message. Laughingly he said, "Do you believe that, Boyle?" Then gazing at the horizon he added, "This is the nicest day we've had in a month." From our bridge we could see the horizon about 20 miles away, due to the curvature of the earth.

"Three hundred and sixty degrees, not a cloud in

the sky, not even a ripple on the ocean. Nothing for us to worry about today," I answered. I relieved Stew of the duty and took charge of the bridge.

My first duty was to check the equipment on the bridge. I checked our signal lights, found them ready for service, then checked the flag bag to see that all the flags had been stored in their proper place.

I placed the telescope in its stand and turned toward the harbor. Nothing seemed amiss there. The transports were all in their assigned places, and the cargo carriers were coughing up their insides to the many small boats that surrounded them like so may young birds being fed by their mothers. On the beach the small boats were unloading as quickly as possible and running back to their mother ships for another helping of whatever was being served. The supplies on the beach were being moved about, trucks running back and forth like armies of worker ants. This was like any other day of military operation, business as usual.

All was serene the first hour of my watch. Many off-duty men were sitting around on the deck enjoying the beautiful day. Those on duty went about their tasks maintaining the equipment they might have to use in case of a fight.

The sea began to get a little more restless, the swells a little larger, we could see a few whitecaps but still no clouds.

On the bridge were the captain, two lookouts, the boatswain's mate, always referred to as "Boats", and I. The captain, sensing trouble, ordered all watertight hatches closed. All equipment that might shift was tied down tightly. All hands who weren't really needed on deck were ordered below to their quarters.

I had overheard the captain requesting the officer of the deck to stay in the wheelhouse. He requested the O.D. to monitor the course and speed orders that he would be giving from the bridge.

The captain then ordered those of us on deck into our foul-weather gear. I thought to myself, what the hell's the matter with him, until I noticed he was already in his gear.

One lookout was sent into the crow's nest 25 feet up the mast, where a lookout can stand with just his head sticking out and his view is increased by about five miles. The other lookout was sent to the stern lookout post. All lookouts were in communication with the bridge by telephone.

The boatswain was all over the deck, checking the waterproof muzzle covers on all the guns, seeing that the swivels were all locked properly so none of them would start swinging as the ship started to pitch and roll, setting up lifelines from bow to stern and to the ladders where anyone on deck might have to go.

I checked the equipment on the bridge. The flag bag was covered with its waterproof cover. I checked to be sure it would not blow off in a wind. I made sure the binoculars were clean and ready for use. There was very little on the flying bridge that could trouble us. Our lights were working properly. Everything was in order. It appeared we were having a big drill of some kind and I had just gotten stuck on the bridge.

It wasn't long after these precautions had taken place that the crow's nest shouted into the phone, "Rainclouds to the southwest, ten to fifteen miles." We could detect fear in his voice. All eyes immediately turned in that direction. I heard the captain gasp as if in silent prayer, "Oh, my God, I don't believe it." From southeast to northwest and as high as we could see into the sky was the most terrifying sight. Night was descending upon us and with it fearful lightning and even from this distance the violent crashing of thunder. Each stroke of thunder sounded like an explosion. When the lightning flashed it was as if the heavens were being torn apart. I waited for a voice to say, "Boyle, your time has come!"

Immediately the captain issued his first order. "Get your ass the hell out of the crow's nest before you get it blown out! Take the forward post." To the wheelhouse, he shouted, "Pass the word to the engine room and the crew's quarters to hang on! We're going to be hit by something, just don't ask me what."

Being pushed ahead of this devastating sight was a wall of howling wind that screeched like a herd of banshees, and rain that felt like knives trying to cut the flesh from the bone.

From the wheelhouse came the O.D.'s voice, "The radar is out and we can't get a damn thing on sonar."

"Shut 'em down. They won't do us a hell of a lot of good in this weather anyway. Put two men on the wheel, you're going to need all the muscle you can get." That's all the captain could say before we were engulfed in a most awe-inspiring and terrific spectacle. Our world was thrown into convulsions. Sheets of water were climbing over the flying bridge. Every time we hit a swell our main deck was under water. The lookouts yelled, "We're lashing ourselves down to keep from being washed overboard." The lightning flashed so close I was sure I could reach out and touch it. I was sure it would destroy us. Close on the heels of the lightning came thunder. Not with a crash but with an explosion that lifted our ship right out of the water like a trout on a fly line, shuddering and shaking before dropping back into the water. I could hear the steel plates of the ship's hull strain as they were twisted to their limits. We were being bounced like a cork upon the raging sea. Each time the lightning flashed, it struck fear into our hearts. Its brightness so illuminated the sky that we thought the end of the world was upon us. The thunder was so deafening that no one on the bridge talked. We were at the mercy of the storm.

The initial fear did not last long. There was too

much to do and it had to be done now. The captain was giving the wheelhouse instructions as to course and speed. Boats and I had one arm wrapped around the light standard, trying to keep our balance. Boats quipped, "Nice knowing you, Boyle. If we make it, I'll buy you one."

I hollered across the ten-foot space that separated us, "As long as we're still afloat we still have a chance." I wouldn't have bet my next check on it, though!

"Hey, Boats, where in hell's the flare gun?" bellowed the captain between cracks of thunder.

"It's in the small arms locker, sir."

The captain hesitated just a few moments and announced, "We're going to need that gun on the bridge."

Now I was worried. The flare gun is used only if there is some grave emergency aboard ship, emergencies where the crew is in danger and may need to be rescued. I scrunched down into my foul-weather gear, hoping the captain couldn't see me. The next order I heard was, "Hey, Boyle, get that flare gun." I knew all along I would have to get it.

The big ships such as transports and cargo ships have passageways that a man can stand up in. Not our patrol craft, however. We were built the same as the larger ships, but were one-tenth the size. A sailor learns early in his career to stoop. No matter what door he goes through, he has to stoop or bump his head. I had to descend the flying bridge down to the wheelhouse and then down to the 'scope-room. Then I went through several three-foot-high passageways in total darkness before I could get to the gun locker and return. My work was cut out for me.

The captain ordered the ship turned so I could get into the wheelhouse without swamping it. I pounded the door. It was yanked open, and I was pulled inside. The door was slapped shut.

"What's going on topside?" all of the men wanted to

know.

"We're catching hell from some kind of a storm," I answered.

"The wind is blowing the rain straight at us, and the lightning and thunder scare the hell out of us." The flying bridge was better than being in the stuffy wheelhouse. The strain on the face of the men on the wheel showed. It took all of their concentration to keep the ship on course. I ripped off my foul-weather gear and piled it in a corner.

I told the O.D. where I was going and asked him, "Sir, if I'm not back in half an hour will you send someone after me?"

He laughed a little and answered, "Don't worry, Boyle, we won't leave you stuck anywhere."

In a far corner of the wheelhouse was a hatch two and a half feet wide. This led to the 'scope room.

"Wish me luck, fellows, here goes nothing," I joked as I quickly opened the hatch and shimmied down to the 'scope room deck. One of the crew slammed the hatch before I had finished talking. The dim light from one red overhead bulb cast an eerie light about the eight-foot 'scope room. Even in these close quarters I had to hang on. The ship was still tossing and rolling wildly. I could imagine what was going on outside. I could hear the thunder crashing. I felt like I was inside a steel drum with someone beating on it.

From this compartment it was necessary for me to crawl through another horizontal tube to the engine room, a tube ten feet long and three feet high with only room to crawl on all fours. After entering I still had to shut the door behind me. This tube had no lights. Closing it was like sealing my own tomb. What I had to do now was to crawl straight ahead in the darkness until I hit my head. Opening the hatch, the engine room crew looked at me as if I were a ghost.

The chief bellowed, "What in hell are you doing

down here?" And in the next breath, with a little more urgency, "What's going on topside?" Again I saw a look of grave concern among the men in the engine room. They put up with engine noise and oily-smelling heat all of the time they were standing watch. In rough weather, it was a hell-hole.

"All hell's breaking loose out there. When the lightning flashes and the thunder crashes it feels like we're being torn apart," I told them.

"Thanks, it feels like that down here, too," replied the chief. "We're getting some damn strange orders down here, I'm glad we know what's happening." The engine crew looked a little shaky, but were very busy and had to stay alert. I had one more tube to go through to reach the crew's quarters.

One of the men hollered over the noise of the engine, "I'll hold the hatch open until you reach the other end. That way you won't hit your head so hard." I scooted through the tube in record time, bounced into the crew's quarters, and looked around. All of the men were at least stripped to the waist. Some were walking around in their shorts and some were in their bunks, too sick to move. The heat and the humidity and the smell of sweating bodies was stifling.

On the deck there were several inches of water sloshing back and forth. The water did its little dance on the deck every time the ship would pitch or roll. I glanced into the head. Some of the men had made it to the trough and were being sick. Some of them didn't make it that far. The deck was covered with a layer of stinking colored water which was sloshing around the head. The men who were sick didn't even care. I decided to stay on the bridge if I ever got back there. The noise of the storm was deafening in the crew's quarters. Every time a crash of thunder hit, it sounded like a sledgehammer being driven against the hull. Inside the ship the sound of twisting steel and the popping of rivets was magnified a hundredfold. I had my arms around the mast when an especially loud crash of thunder hit. As the ship rolled to port, I felt the mast twisting in my arms. I became so frightened that I quickly headed for the gun locker, grabbed the flare gun and ammunition and reversed course.

Going through the crew's quarters I told my watch relief, "Lee, you don't have to relieve me on the bridge. I'm wet already; no use you getting wet, too." I didn't tell him I was afraid to stay below. He didn't feel well and thought I was doing him a favor, so he agreed. I was happy to be heading back to the bridge and made record time getting there.

"How are things going below?" the O.D. asked, when I popped through the hatch. When I explained the conditions in the crew's quarters, he said, "Those poor devils. There's going to be a lot more of them sick before this thing is over." I hurriedly got into my foul-weather gear again and climbed up to the flying bridge.

Before the captain could say anything, I spoke up. "Captain, I'm all wet already, Lee is sick and he's willing to let me take his watch. Is it all right with you, sir?"

He smiled and answered, "I'm staying up here for the duration of the storm; if you want to keep me company it's all right with me." I sometimes wonder if he was scared too.

We were still patrolling our assigned area, trying to keep as close to the six-mile stretch as we could under these crazy conditions. We were pitching and rolling; water was still splashing over the flying bridge. Every time a flash of lightning exploded, I squinted my eyes.

The loudspeaker was hooked up on the bridge so we could hear radio messages from the other ships. Even if we felt alone, we knew by the messages being sent that other ships were having more trouble than we were. One in trouble was a sub-chaser which was even smaller than the patrol craft. This ship not only had most of its electrical equipment knocked out, they also had engine trouble and could only produce ten knots speed. They were taking on water and if their pumps stopped they would have to abandon ship.

The code books and all the messages had been put into a weighted bag to be thrown over the side if they had to abandon ship. We felt sorry for the men on the sub-chasers and minesweepers. They were a part of our task unit. There were eight ships in our task unit: three P.C.'s, three S.C.'s and two minesweepers. We knew they were taking a beating because we were. One of the minesweepers had already requested permission to return to the harbor. No O.K. had been given yet.

Boats and I had our searchlights working the water in front of us. There was a great deal of floating debris that either had washed off the ship's deck or had broken away from its mooring. We tried to steer clear of the debris.

Little note of time was made by the men on the bridge. It had been midnight since one in the afternoon. We finally received a message that lifted our spirits. All ships on picket duty were to return to the harbor and find mooring for the duration of the storm. Immediately, the captain ordered our navigator to the wheelhouse.

It was only moments later that we heard through the voice tube, "Lt. McDermott reporting, sir." And with a lilt of laughter, he added, "Want me to take you kids home?" The captain let out a hearty laugh. He knew we were on our way to a safe mooring place.

The captain told McDermott, "I'm going to give some course and speed orders from the flying bridge because of all the crap that's floating around."

McDermott answered, "I'll head you in the general direction and when we hit the harbor lights she's all yours."

The captain called back, "Thanks, Mac. Get us that far and we'll take it the rest of the way."

We couldn't just turn the ship and head for the harbor. We would have the storm at our back and lose all control of the steering. We had to zig-zag as slowly as we could and still keep the ship under control. Our searchlights were picking out quite an array of floating debris in the water now. One of the more dangerous objects was a floating dry dock. When Boats first spotted it with his light, he thought it was another ship.

A floating dry dock is a series of steel tanks which can be filled with water so the dock will sink and a small boat can go into the center. The tanks are then pumped full of air, forcing the water out. The dry dock will then rise up so the ship can be worked on. That way repairs can be made without the small ships going onto the beach or land docks. This dock bearing down on us looked like a three-story building ready to shove us out of the way. The captain changed course in a hurry. We passed within 30 feet of it. "That was too close for comfort. I'm goddamn glad we spotted it in time," sighed Boats.

After picking our way through tons of floating junk, we spotted a harbor light. The captain called down the voice tube, "We got a light, Mac. Come up long enough to identify." That's how long Mac stayed on the flying bridge. He had come up without his foul-weather gear, so within minutes he was soaked. But he did determine for us that the light we spotted was the east light. He then set our course to enter the harbor. The captain slapped Mac on his wet back, "Thanks, Mac. Get into some dry clothes. We'll take it from here."

We were able to find the harbor channel without any trouble. Getting through the channel was like plowing through a batch of bread dough. It seemed like all the water in the harbor was trying to get out at once. It felt like we would move ahead 20 feet and get pushed back 15. The swells from the harbor were as bad as those on the open sea. We passed the natural breakwater. The thunder and lightning were as bad as on the open sea, and the rain still beat on us as if it were trying to drive us out of the area. Being in the shelter of the harbor, we were safe from the raging seas. We didn't have to hang on so tightly to stay on our feet. Our job now was to find something to tie up to. When the lightning flashed, we could see many of the larger ships swinging on their anchor chains tugging to get loose. We could not tie up to any large ship, for if we did we would be crushed if it started to roll. We needed to find something closer to our size. We started to traverse the harbor at a slow speed. As there was still quite a bit of debris floating around, Boats and I kept the searchlights busy. We spotted an L.S.T. about fifty yards to starboard and headed for it. When we were within hailing distance, the captain grabbed the bullhorn and requested permission to tie up to them. Their bullhorn gave us our reply, "We've already got a destroyer tied up on the other side. If we let you tie up we'll all be smashed." So, the search went on.

Like picket duty, we steamed back and forth, only in a much shorter path. The thunder was still deafening, but here the lightning was a blessing. Every flash lit up the harbor so we could see what we were up against. A brilliant flash silhouetted an anchor buoy about a quarter mile away. We steered for it. These anchor buoys are placed in harbors away from the docks and the shore, so large ships could tie up to them and be unloaded. They are about 20 feet across and made up of hollow drums banded together with concrete poured over to make a solid deck. Anchored to the bottom of the harbor, they have a large ring in the center for the ships' lines.

The captain explained, "Boats, I'm going to pass close enough for you to jump and grab the ring."

Boats answered without hesitation, "Yes sir!"

The captain called the lookouts to the bridge and

explained again, "I'm going to pass as close as I can to that buoy. Boats will jump for the ring. When we back up, you men throw the lines so we can tie up. Boyle will handle the light."

We were all a little nervous. Boats took up his position outside the deck rail. The lookouts were in position with the lines ready to go and I was on the light. The captain made his approach, scraping some paint as he hit it. Boats made a nice four-point landing, catching the ring. We went past the buoy about 50 yards and had to back up to throw the lines. They went in a perfect arc and he had them tied down quickly. We all heaved a sigh of relief.

We were now snuggled up to a safe mooring and Boats could climb over the rail onto the deck. The captain hollered, "That was a hell of a nice piece of work, Boats. Well done."

The lightning flashed and the thunder crashed, but being safely moored, the storm no longer seemed so threatening.

The captain told the four of us to report to his cabin. He looked pretty well tired out when we entered. He smiled, "You men did one hell of a job." Handing each a half pint of medical brandy, he said, "You men have been topside for 20 hours. Drink this and stay in your sacks until you wake up." Then with a big grin on his face, he said, "Thanks, fellows."

Selection Five

Uncle Eli

by Rose Rothenburg

UNCLE ELI WAS A CHARACTER. HE WAS MY
father's oldest brother and the second son in a
family of six whose members differed from one another
in many ways. But Eli was really different. For one
thing, he was a bachelor. When I was a little girl of six
or seven and Uncle Eli was in his mid-forties, his single
state was already accepted by the family as not very
likely to change.

True, there was a story circulating about how close
to matrimony he had once come. With his slim, straight
carriage, wavy brown hair, expressive eyes and regular
features, he certainly was not unattractive. In fact, in
his mid-thirties he was considered quite a catch. To the
young widow, Ruth, he seemed quite a likely prospect.
The death of her ailing first husband had released Ruth
from years of dutiful attendance upon him. Now, staring
into the third decade of her life, she turned her energy
and attention to finding a new husband. The introductions had come about through a remote relative who cer-

tainly must have known my uncle only superficially. Though he had never looked upon marriage with favor, Uncle Eli was smitten with Ruth. She was fair to look upon and one could not ask for a more refined and cultured lady. Uncle Eli noted with satisfaction, also, that she was gainfully employed as a milliner.

He pressed the courtship with ardor and in short order they were engaged. They discussed wedding plans with pleasure and care. They agreed upon their future living arrangements. Things were hopping along quite smoothly. It was the honeymoon discussion that brought the courtship to a grinding halt. You see, the bride-to-be dearly wanted to honeymoon in nearby Atlantic City, which in the twenties was the place to go. Uncle Eli balked. It was one thing to get married but quite another to incur such an unnecessary expense.

Not that he couldn't afford it. My father and uncle had both labored hard at their trade as metalsmiths. But while my father was weighed down with wife and kids and had not a penny in the bank, Uncle Eli had already amassed a small fortune.

You may well question that a metalsmith, even an unmarried one, could have acquired a sizable nest egg so early in life. I assure you it was perfectly possible if you lived as my uncle did. He was a boarder and had his room on the third floor rear in a neighborhood that had seen better days in the past—the very distant past. After a time he figured that he was paying too much for board. He was a delicate eater and could hardly do justice to the hearty meals served by his "missus." He became instead a steady customer at the local kosher restaurant. Here he could order, and pay for, just what he could eat. Moreover, it became clear that if he started his day a little later he could easily make do with two meals rather than three. The arrangement proved so satisfactory that he continued in this way for thirty-some years, at which time the restaurant went out of business.

Uncle Eli was a dapper man and extremely meticulous about his person. His shirts were always pure white, at least until they yellowed a bit with age. His dark serge suit was always well pressed and clean. It did not yellow with the passage of time, but took on a shine that competed with the gloss he maintained on his high-button shoes. In the summer months he sported spotless white buckskin oxfords—the same pair year after year. His straw hat was worn at a rakish angle and, rain or shine, he was never without an umbrella.

Uncle Eli felt no great need for entertainment or divertissement, though he did indulge at times and pay the ten cent admission to a movie. Occasionally, too, he walked the few miles into town and climbed to the topmost gallery to attend a matinee concert at the Academy of Music.

So, you see, it was impossible for Uncle Eli not to have acquired some money. Atlantic City was certainly not out of reach financially. It simply made no sense to him to spend money on a honeymoon. Nevertheless, he was not an unreasonable man; Ruth was very desirable and he was more than willing to compromise. He told his lady love that they would marry and that he would bankroll *her* visit to Atlantic City for a few days and *he* would remain behind in Philadelphia and wait for her. Upon such stunning revelation of what life with my uncle would be, Ruth's dream of marriage and security exploded. She broke the engagement forthwith.

Well, so much for romance. Anyhow, it certainly must have soured Uncle Eli on marriage because he remained a lifetime bachelor.

Uncle Eli was sociable to a degree. He visited our house often but never stayed very long. Now, our house was just as clean as any other that had half a dozen kids dashing about. Even so, when Uncle Eli put in an appearance my mother quickly surveyed the parlor and removed any appearance of dirt. But Uncle Eli, before seating himself, extricated his white handkerchief and with a few swift flourishes dusted the chair that was offered him. Only then did he carefully lower himself to the edge of the chair, hook his umbrella on his arm, remove his hat and with the cuff of his jacket give it a quick swipe and place it on his knee. He was ready to visit.

My parents raised us to respect our elders and asking visiting relatives for anything was certainly frowned upon. In the case of my uncle there was an exception. If it happened that he visited on a warm summer evening, my father might hint broadly that it would be nice for the children to have an ice cream treat. That was our signal to begin pleading with my uncle for money. Uncle Eli would sit like a block of wood while my father laughingly encouraged our efforts. Sometimes our wheedling paid off and my uncle doled out three cents each for a single-dip cone. Having succeeded this far, we usually explained that just a penny more would get us a sprinkling of chocolate jimmies over the ice cream. But he would protest that we wanted the moon and would shoo us from his presence. We considered it a victory anyway because we recognized that Uncle Eli had limits.

The years were not kind to Uncle Eli. He lost a good bit of his hearing and he became even more reclusive. My father and he could communicate during his infrequent visits only because my father was blessed with sturdy lungs and the will to use them. My mother, after a few attempts at polite conversation, would escape to the kitchen with her hands over her ears. By this time we children had outgrown the game of trying to pry money from Uncle Eli and he generally ignored us.

As the years piled up, my uncle's eccentricities became a matter of great concern to my father and his sisters. Eccentric behavior had deteriorated into plain craziness. His earlier attention to cleanliness of person gave way to complete indifference about his attire. It became ever more apparent that the shirts were not being laundered regularly, and the suit had long outlived its respectability. The shoes, dull and scuffed, needed to be reheeled. The handkerchief that was still whipped out to dust a chair had done duty too long. He had long since been persuaded to turn over his financial affairs to a nephew by marriage whom he trusted, and he was never in want. Nevertheless, it took the combined efforts of my father and his sisters to convince him from time to time to buy a new wardrobe.

Uncle Eli was well into his eighties when he was finally prevailed upon to turn over his remaining assets to the Jewish Home for the Aged in return for lifetime care. Death claimed him there at age 93.

I often think about the strange life my uncle lived and wonder what story I would now be telling had he embarked on that honeymoon trip so long ago.

SELECTION SIX

ESCAPE TO FREEDOM
by Rose Saposnek

1. MY EARLY LIFE IN RUSSIA

BARDITCHEV WAS A CHARMING LITTLE FARM town in Russia of about two thousand farmers and their families. Jews and Christians lived peacefully side by side. Acres of wheat and corn fields skirted the town.

Main Street on Sunday was quite lively as the farmers and their families gathered to sell their wares and socialize. Dressed in my Sunday best, I waited with Mama impatiently as Papa harnessed the family horse and hitched the horse to the wagon. We then drove to Main Street, where we were greeted warmly and socialized. Papa usually bought me a trinket and, best of all, he bought me some *saharni maroz* (ice cream).

Later in the afternoon we would ride far out in the country passing farm after farm, passing Papa's old wooden one-room school house and the water hole further down where Papa and his school friends swam. Sitting so high up on the wagon between my parents, I could see patches of watermelon and cantaloupes nestled in the fields.

But too soon trouble started and anti-Semitism reared its ugly head. Papa then decided to leave for America and would send for Mama and me. The family was saddened but agreed that was the best plan.

I became more dear to my grandparents as they remarked how closely I resembled their son—my father. Grandpa was a tall and sinewy man, a hardworking and quiet person. He had sandy hair and blue eyes, eyes that had a twinkle only for me. I spent most of my time following him around the farm after Papa left. I remember my grandfather milking a cow. As I stood watching and listening to the squirting of the milk into the pail, I stuck my hands into the pail, feeling the warmth of the milk and washing my face with it. Grandpa laughed and gently scolded me.

Although the horses frightened me and kept me at a distance, I loved all the other animals on the farm. Once I was brave enough to cuddle a baby chick while the mother hen protested loudly.

Grandma was a no-nonsense and serious person. She was dark-complected, with brown, serious eyes. Although Grandma was only in her mid-forties, she was quite wrinkled. Housekeeping and cooking for seven of us kept her busy.

2. ESCAPE

The year 1917 in Odessa was getting very scary. People gathering in groups in the streets were exchanging stories of atrocities and killings that they heard were happening in nearby towns. I overheard Mama talking to neighbors, asking each other where would they go, where would they hide if suddenly the Cossacks appeared.

I remember being awakened one morning by shooting and crying outside. I ran to the bedroom window and as I looked out, I could see soldiers with guns guarding our neighbor's house.

"Mama, Mama," I cried.

She came running, holding her hands to her chest.

"Look," I said, pointing to the window.

We stood terrified, watching the Cossacks in their gray uniforms and black caracul hats pulling out our neighbors, who were struggling and crying out in bewilderment. Their six children ranging from two to thirteen years of age, some of them my playmates, were also dragged along to the rear of the house, where they were all lined against the wall of the house and riddled with machine-gun fire—all eight of them.

Quickly we ran to a neighbor's house. There they led us down to the cellar, where families were sitting huddled together. A single candle was the only light. When guns sounded closer, Mama decided to brave the way to her friend's house.

I remember holding tightly to Mama's hand as we said our good-byes to the neighbors, and hurried out of the cellar into the street. The streets, once so beautifully lined with lacy trees, with people bustling about through fashionable shops, couples holding hands and looking longingly into jewelry store windows at sparkling diamonds, were now in ruins. I saw charred trees, gaping store windows, crumbling buildings and dismembered bodies lying in full view.

We arrived breathlessly at the house where Mama's friend lived, only to be stopped at the foot of the stairs by two young, sadistic looking soldiers.

"Halt," they commanded, one pointing a gun at us while the other demanded money. Mama had sewn all of her savings in the back of her blouse. Picking me up with trembling hands and holding me tightly, she was thinking that if she were killed, I might as well be killed also.

"Hand over all of your money, Jew," the Cossack demanded. Mama denied that she had money. He began to search her, almost reaching the back of her blouse, when the other soldier becoming bored with the whole thing, put down his gun and said, "Ah, leave them go and find others."

Mama weakly led me up the stairs to find all of the family slaughtered. As we heard someone walking up the stairs, Mama quickly pulled me under a bloody blanket that covered a dead body. She smeared our faces and hair with blood.

"Hush," Mama whispered.

Soon soldiers arrived.

"They are all dead," one said as he tapped Mama with the butt of his gun to make sure. When we heard them leave, we then ran to a Christian friend of Mama's. She not only offered us shelter, but also told us of a man that helped people like us cross the border to freedom. My mother took this chance.

◊ ◊ ◊

It was midnight as my mother woke me gently. As she dressed me, she told me in a hushed tone to be very quiet. It was dark and I was too sleepy to ask questions. Mama picked me up and carried me quietly out into the darkness. We were going to steal across the Russian border. I must have fallen asleep again, for the next thing I remember we were waiting near a huge body of water—the Black Sea. The full moon outlined a man rowing a boat toward us. The lapping of the waves was the only sound in the silent night.

Mama whispered to me. "This nice man," she pointed, "will row us across the sea. We must be very quiet," she cautioned again. As he helped us into the tiny boat, I took a dislike to the stranger. He smelled bad and he had a leering smile. No words were spoken as we got into the row boat. The boat rocked dangerously as he stepped in and sat down facing us. Picking up the oars, he smiled his leering smile at us. I could feel Mama's body tense. It was cold and dark, the moon only reflected the blackness of the Black Sea. I buried my face with my hands so as not to see him.

"Hey, *malinka jevitsky*" (little girl), he sneered gleefully, sensing my distress, "if you make one move, the boat will tip over and we'll all drown in this black sea, ha, ha," he laughed wildly. The man was drunk. Mama drew me closer to her as she quietly started to pray.

"Dear God," I heard her say, "please help me through this ordeal as you have helped me before, please for my child's sake." Mama always talked to God, but it frightened me to see her cry.

"Please, Mama," I pleaded, "don't cry."

Then like a miracle, the man changed.

"Don't worry, woman," he said gruffly, "I'll get you on land." He was quiet the rest of the trip.

It was still dark as we reached the shore. As he helped us out of the boat, Mama asked the man, "Where are we now?" He shrugged his shoulder and said, "You are in Rumania. There are farms nearby, the rest is up to you." He took his money and rowed away into the darkness. I began to cry. It was so cold and dark. Mama firmly took my hand and pulled me along. It was getting lighter as we walked and soon we heard dogs barking. A farmer being alerted by his barking dogs was standing by his farm with a gun. We must have been a pitiful sight as we approached him. Without questioning us, he led us into the house, where his wife was preparing breakfast.

Once more Mama's prayers were answered.

SELECTION SEVEN

JEFFERSON BARRACKS, MISSOURI

by John Strong

JEFFERSON BARRACKS, MISSOURI, OUTSIDE OF St. Louis, where Robert E. Lee, U. S. Grant, Stonewall Jackson and Sherman, fresh out of West Point, were once stationed.

The mail truck sped through the gates of the Jefferson Barracks reservation. No guards were at the gate. Bill Bee, Ford Smith and I, John Strong, were buried among the mail bags.

I raised myself up to catch my first look at J.B. I saw several red brick buildings, a large parade ground, all foreboding-looking, and a tent city on the left. However, the thing that caught my attention was the large number of young fellows, teenagers mostly, like an overgrown Boys Town. Some had uniforms, others wore parts of uniforms, but mostly they were in street clothes. Many were drilling on the parade ground. "Left, right, left, right," was the cadence. Some were drilling with broom sticks, of all things. I didn't like the looks of all this at all—and no airplanes at all. Wasn't this the Air Corps?

The driver of the mail truck finally slammed on the brakes and yelled, "Get out. This is where you report in. Stand in front of this building until someone comes around." With that, he was gone in a cloud of dust.

Bob, Ford and I were lucky to jump out before the little snot drove off. Suddenly, the shriek of a siren pierced the air. We looked at each other, wondering what that was for; maybe a fire. All at once, a stampede of teenagers came thundering across the parade ground. Caught up in the hysteria, we started to sprint along with the others. Then the mob slowed down, and we saw a long line forming. It snaked across the parade grounds, down along a wall, and entered a large gray building.

"What's going on here?" I asked a fellow who had on a khaki shirt, overseas cap, and street pants.

"It's chow time," he replied. "New here, eh? I hope you have a strong stomach."

We finally worked our way into the gigantic mess hall and into the chow line. Five thousand men ate here in shifts, I was told. Needless to say, the three of us were starved. The K.P. crew measured out baked beans like they were gold nuggets, about twelve to a guy. We got some chicken soup, two slices of bread, a small piece of steak, some sliced peaches and coffee.

Believe it or not, we now carried our trays through a toilet to the far side of the mess hall. There were a few veterans in line. Right behind me was a big sergeant in a clean new uniform. I walked past a water dispenser that was leaking like mad, making a puddle on the floor. Suddenly my feet went out from under me and, as I slid in the water, the tray went up in the air. The beans and peaches went all over the sergeant's clean uniform, and I went skidding along the floor like a base runner going into second.

The sergeant let out a yell as though he was scalded. "Big dumb recruit, didn't you see the water? Look at my new uniform! I hope I get you on the drill field, Buster!"

I hoped he wouldn't get me! Several men sitting nearby were laughing their heads off. "Hey, look at Ty Cobb going into second."

"This is the funniest thing that has happened in this hell-hole. We needed a good laugh."

Finally, I got up, looked at my soggy green gabardine suit and tried to pick up the tray and dishes.

I sat beside Bill and Ford, who wanted to share their meal. I wouldn't see it. I was disgusted.

"This soup is awful," protested Ford. "They could have made the chicken run through the water a couple of times instead of once. The steak is like show leather, and my spoon just dissolved in the coffee."

Bill Bee, ever the optimist, was eating the slop as though it was caviar. He even had a smile on his face.

So my first meal in the army mess hall was a big zero. My sides were caving in, I was so hungry. I had some gum, so I chewed two sticks and that was my meal at J.B.

As we returned to the building where the mail truck driver had deposited us, Ford Smith wiped his face with his handkerchief. This gave me an opening for a little joke—we needed one.

"Remember when you used that handkerchief last, Ford," I teased.

Ford, who was a very clean fellow, exploded. "That damn pigeon crap—and I'm wiping my face in it—oh, no!"

Some short jerk with temporary white corporal stripes pinned on his sleeves screamed at us. "Why did you leave this place and go to chow? Now you'll have to drag your cots up three flights of stairs."

He led us to a room where another teenager in a green fatigue jacket, street pants and bare feet was reading a comic book—the reading habit here at J.B., evidently.

Very much irritated, he growled, "I thought all the new recruits had gone through."

Our temporary corporal replied, "These three musketeers couldn't obey orders so they were gone in the mess line to sample our wonderful chow. I'll bet they won't be too anxious to sweat out the line after eating our cattle food. Anyway, they need a blanket and a cot."

The barefoot Huck Finn led us to another room, in the center of which was a huge wooden box. Then he took an axe and began to knock the sides off the crate with a vengeance, swinging the axe like an expert lumberjack. Finally, all the boards and slats fell off, revealing a mammoth store of brown wool blankets. Sweating profusely, Huck Finn now grabbed a blanket and pitched it to Bill Bee, then one to Ford and one to me. I almost asked Ford to loan him his pigeon hankie to wipe the sweat off.

Next the "corporal" marched us to another room, where stacks of folded iron cots were piled. "Take one and lug it up to the third floor. We don't have any mattresses now; we'll have some tomorrow."

Carrying the cot and blankets up three flights of stairs was quite a trick. Actually we dragged the cots.

This was our first night at Jefferson Barracks.

SELECTION EIGHT

WRONGS MY MOTHER BROUGHT ME

by Gina Wilcox

NO! SHE DIDN'T BRING ME ANY WRONGS. She screamed and yelled and hit out whenever life got unbearable. When there was no escape from her confinement to all of us—to Papa, to us, to her own large rough family. No one there to complain to, ever. She had probably married papa entirely against their wishes. Pa was an intellectual, a high class someone, and they were railroad workers, construction guys, who would later become cops and milkmen. She had better keep her mouth shut, cry alone and try to deal with me, who, unfortunately for all of us, became "Papa's girl." I don't know how old I was when I finally realized that I was never going to get along with Mama. That there would be no harmony between us. That I could never please her. That it was entirely a matter of whatever a baby calls Fate or Luck. It would always hang on Mama's mood, how it had gone with her that day. Papa had con-

sumption, smoked cigarettes, drank wine with his Zora
friends, a men's chorus of which he was president. Papa
was adored by all his friends and I can see by the pictures in their album that the ladies liked flirting with
Pa. In fact, it begins to dawn on me that the reason no
one looks quite comfortable in the posed wedding picture was Mama's need to rush to the altar. Was I the
invisible villain? Was Papa trapped? Did he get even by
his neglect? Was my life this poor woman's bitter
reward? All could be. From my point of view, feeling it
backwards, I remember that I finally stopped trying to
get through to Mama, that it did not work. I would have
to take a position in life which kept these two people
apart in my life, to deal with each one separately. I suppose this process came gradually, as all knowledge that
stays.

I was about eight when I no longer tried to understand Mama or to consider that she might understand
me. Both Nettie and I tried to do exactly what Mama
said. Exactly was easy, it was doing anything by yourself that might be punishable. One time, when I was six
and Nettie was four, Mama left us all alone in the flat
for the whole morning. It was exciting being alone. I was
the smart sister. Smart? Well, the one who was always
looking to find out... to do whatever there was to do...to
make nice, if possible. Now our mama was forever cleaning our house. It was the serious business of each day.
Our mama scrubbed the floor on her hands and knees.
There was a pail, a wooden scrub brush with a nice
shape and yellow bristles all bent over to one side, and
some old damp rags under the sink. The thing that I was
absolutely sure of in my mama, if nothing else, was that
Cleaning The House Was Important.

So. We would surprise her! We hauled out the
equipment. It took some doing to get the pail full of
water from the high sink, and down to the floor. We
rubbed the brown soap on to the brush, swished the

water around, scrubbed, then tried to rinse the bubbles away after the soap scrubbing. You did that by putting all the rags into the pail of water, and then swishing them over the scrubbed part. Except the rags got too heavy and big to twist most of the water out, so that instead of rinsing the soap away and sopping up the wet part, our scrubbed spots got soppier. It must have taken all the time Mama was gone. Hours. Nettie and I were exhausted and we had only done half the kitchen. And then I remembered about the last part, the laying on of newspapers. I had watched Mama doing this many times and knew that the papers were stacked in the back porch. Now I wondered if she did this because the floor was wet? Or to keep it clean after the scrubbing? Or because of dirty galoshes? Whatever it was, it was certain that laying the newspapers was a finishing touch. So we did that. I could see that our floor was not coming out like Mama's, but I couldn't figure out why. Throughout our heavy labor, dragging the big pail from spot to spot, trying to get those rags to be manageable, watching the soap skitter about, Nettie and I were happy that we had hit on something Mama would bless us for, so it was worth the labor. It was a grown-up, useful activity, we were Good Girls! When she came through the front door, through the parlor, the dining room and into the kitchen, we were beaming with surprise for her.

"Oh My God!" she screamed, "what have you done?" She began whirling about in a frenzy of motion—putting things in her arms down, picking up stuff off the floor, moving faster and faster, her voice getting more shrill and powerful in curses and yells. Nettie and I were dazed. Frozen into stone ears and eyes. Sister ultimately squished up her face into a wailing bawl and hung on to my bloomer dress. I remained rigid, watching Mama whirling and raging. It was so startling, there was no time to be offended by it. Mama's anger had its own being, whatever the cause was, so I could disconnect from it. As she whirled and yelled, picked up the pail and dumped it into the toilet, swooped up the puddled newspapers we had so carefully laid down, she took a big swipe at me, then another which made Nettie scream louder with fear. Not me. I realized that this was something for which I could not find the connection. The same something that I had experienced many times, in different scenes. There was no explaining some things between Mama and me, and this was one of the most serious times. Yes, she beat me. She even slapped Nettie's bottom, Nettie, her little sweet one. From that time on, I knew better how to be the other to Mama's storms. I stood still, and remained silent. No matter what the situation. Even those ugly probing questions grownups pierce children with, I would remain silent. Beat me? Slap me? Didn't make any difference. I had learned the way to keep my dignity and my own counsel. I could never lie. I still can't lie. I stayed silent and sad. Sad for Mama. In 1921 Mama had no allies. She had no release from the hopeless balance of her private world. Mama was not lucky. Later, when I was ten, I confessed to Mama how much I wished I could sing the role of Kathy in "The Student Prince," the operetta my father's singing society would produce that spring. I knew all the words to all the songs. Mama just looked at me and said, "Wish in one hand and shit in the other, see what comes out first."

Selection Nine

Mom

by Louis Doshay

WHY DO I HAVE SUCH A HARD TIME WRITING about you? After all, you've been gone for thirty-four years now. So why does it still bring tears to my eyes? Maybe if I just imagine that I'm really talking to you, maybe then I can put it all down. Maybe then I can get the words out. And who knows? Maybe you can really hear me.

So why the tears? Is it because I still haven't let go? Yes, that might be part of it. You left us too soon. You died. Why do I have such a hard time saying that word? I guess it's too final, and I'm not done with you yet. And I never had time to do those things for you that I promised. I know you told me that I never would, but that just makes it hurt all the more. You were right when you said I would find a wife to do things for and give things to. But you were wrong when you said that then I would forget you.

And it hurts me that you never got the real joy that you deserved. You never saw two of your grandchildren, David and Denise. Everyone says that Denise looks a lot like you did at her age. She's as beautiful as her sister, Doreen, but she has a *zoftik* figure, more like yours, and she has your round face. And you should see how tall David has grown. I'm four inches taller than Pop was, and David is four inches taller than I am. He is almost six feet tall.

But I ramble on about this and that, and I still don't talk about us. Surely our unfinished business has more to do with you and me. Remember when we were moving to California? I was fifteen then, and I was the navigator. I plotted our progress on the maps the Auto Club had given us, and gave Pop the directions for each change of highway. I can't remember what it was about, but you hit me. I got very angry at that, and I got out of the car and ran away. I was too proud to come back, but I didn't really want to get lost. So I walked down the side of the main highway toward Los Angeles. In about half an hour Pop found me, and I let him persuade me to get into the car. Pop was good at letting me get off the hook without my having to lose face.

That reminds me of that other time I ran away. I think I was about eight years old. Pop, you, and I were walking in Cratona Park after supper. I'm not really sure why you hit me that time either, but I suppose I could have been bugging you to buy me a penny's worth of "Polly" seeds from one of those walking salesboys who were always selling things in the park on summer evenings. I really was a stubborn kid, and I never gave up easily. When you hit me, I ran away and shouted I was never coming home again. Pop chased me for a little while, but he didn't have a chance of catching me. He was in his forties, and a little on the heavy side. I went to the other side of the park, near Fulton Avenue, and I sat down and felt sorry for myself. And I cried. You sent my brother, Manny, to find me. By the time he did, it was well after dark. Manny didn't waste time being diplomatic. He grabbed me by the scruff of the neck and took me home.

But those incidents are not the ones that bothered me the most. There were others that really hurt. Like when I was in the fourth grade, and I brought home my report card. I had one "B" and the rest all "A's." You told me, "So what good is that. Your brother, Carl, got straight 'A's' when he was your age. And what good did it do? He still quit college to marry that girl. And you'll do the same thing. You'll meet a girl, and you'll quit school and get married."

"No, I won't," I shouted. "You'll see. I'll finish college. You'll see." Well, you saw that I was right, and you were only two-thirds right. Oh, I met Sylvia and got married all right, but I didn't quit school until after I graduated. I didn't even quit when Doreen was born over a year before my graduation. I didn't even consider quitting, and Sylvia never suggested it. Not even the time when all we had in the house to eat for three days was pancakes and beans. Yes, what you had said made me determined to prove you wrong, but what a price I paid inside when I was little for that determination.

But I don't blame you any longer for that. I know that you gave me determination the best way you knew. Yet I still have to tell you that it hurt. I made sure I didn't make that mistake with my children, but I made my share of other mistakes.

And why don't I remember you giving me a hug? I don't remember hugging you. Those two things still hurt.

I remember the last time Sylvia, little Doreen and I came to see you before you died. Your hair was completely white in front and around the sides, even though you were only fifty-six. It framed your face beautifully, and I told you how great you looked. How were we to know you were right when you said you would die soon?

I love you.

SELECTION TEN

A LOST SOUL

by Rose Rothenberg

I SEE KATE AS SHE WAS THEN IN THE BLOOM OF her youth, yet so oddly old beyond her years. Her lustrous, red, wavy hair was worn shoulder length, parted on the side, brushed away from her rather plain face and held in place with a barrette. Stylish tortoiseshell glasses failed to hide the pain reflected in her pale brown eyes. A sprinkling of freckles spotted her forehead and extended into the areas just under the eyes.

Kate was a pleasant, soft-spoken, agreeable girl, but often seemed distant, as if only a part of her were involved with the present. Quite often, too, when her features relaxed in a lovely, wide-mouthed smile, her eyes remained sad, remote.

The sadness I perceived in her spoke to a certain melancholy of my own spirit that surfaced now and then, and I was drawn to her. But our friendship was slow to mature.

At the time she became a part of our social group

she was living with her sister and brother-in-law, and I wondered about her parents. The reserve she maintained, however, kept me from making personal inquiries.

Kate joined in our activities with apparent pleasure. We hiked in the Wissahickon, attended plays and concerts, came together for Saturday night gatherings at one or the other of our homes. Kate and I occasionally double-dated. She was a well-liked and accepted member of our little clique.

While many of us were still struggling to rise above the Depression and were constantly in search of better jobs, Kate was secure in her job as bookkeeper. To the unobservant she was successfully functioning in the business world as well as being socially active and involved. I knew somehow that she was not as carefree as the façade she presented would indicate, but I could not guess what her problems might be. Her story emerged haltingly in snatches of exchanged confidences over a long period of time.

Her father was a coarse, bullying man who verbally abused his wife, and beat Kate and her sister for the slightest misbehavior. The mother, a timid soul who lived in fear of her husband, could offer her daughters little love of comfort and no protection from the father's sudden rages. The only kindness Kate knew as she was growing up came from her sister, Mary, older than she by half a dozen years. But Mary married at a very young age to escape the harshness of life at home, leaving Kate quite alone.

The mother's deliverance came with sickness and merciful death. Through most of high school Kate continued to live with her father and absorbed his abuse as best she could. When conditions became intolerable for Kate, Mary moved Kate to her own household. It was not long before the father also died, perhaps a victim of his own meanness.

Kate was afflicted with guilt because of her inadequacy in alleviating her mother's tortured existence. She was further burdened with the hatred she bore her father, even in death, which she could not throw off. Nor could she accept her hatred as a reasonable response to the tragedy of her childhood.

One Sunday in spring, I realized I had not seen Kate in several weeks. I called her and suggested a visit to Horticultural Hall in Fairmount Park. She told me quite curtly that she could not join me, thanked me for calling and hung up. Several times after that I called and met with a similar response. I learned that she had withdrawn from our other friends as well. Perhaps she had made other friendships, I told myself. Weeks went by and Kate did not appear among us. Well, I would have to forget her.

But one day her sister Mary called me and asked if I would come to the house to see Kate.

"Why doesn't Kate invite me?" I asked.

There was a short silence and then Mary said, "I know she would like to see you but she is not well and cannot call you."

"What's wrong with her?" I asked needlessly, for I guessed her illness was not physical.

"Kate is depressed. She has not gone to work for the past week. She needs to talk to someone. Won't you come?"

I had no idea what good it would do but of course I would go. I walked the mile to her house quickly and was greeted at the door by Mary.

"I didn't want to say much over the phone. Kate is upstairs," she said. "She really worries me. She's just been lying on her bed looking up at the ceiling. I can't get a word out of her. She won't even come downstairs to eat. She hasn't bathed in days. I didn't tell her I called you. Please see what you can do."

I climbed the stairs rather fearfully. Kate was indeed lying on her back, her eyes fixed blankly on the ceiling. I sat on the bed beside her and greeted her. "You sick or something? What are you doing in bed?"

Kate looked at me wearily. "What brings you here? How come you didn't call first?"

"I did," I lied. "Mary told me you weren't feeling well. You don't have a cold, do you?" "No, I don't have a cold," she answered, and remained in the same unmoving position.

"Well, then, get dressed and let's go. There's a good movie at the Majestic."

"I don't feel like a movie," Kate said in an irritated voice.

"I feel like dying," she said flatly. "Go yourself; don't bother about me, I'm not worth it."

"Maybe you're right, but it's awfully hot up here. If you don't feel like a movie, let's take a walk and stop for ice cream."

"Look, don't waste your time; I'm not going anywhere," Kate responded angrily.

"Neither am I, till you get out of bed," I retorted with more spirit than I felt. "You look awful. Wash your face and comb your hair and let's get out of here."

My heart was beating wildly and I didn't know what to say or do next. Surprisingly, Kate got out of bed and went into the bathroom. I waited and when she came out she snatched up her purse and started down the stairs. I followed. At the bottom of the stairs she called into the kitchen, "I'm going out for awhile. I don't know when I'll be back." Mary came to the kitchen door and threw me a grateful look.

We walked the several miles to the movie without exchanging more than a dozen words. After the show I said I was hungry, and Kate did not protest when I suggested stopping for a hamburger. She ate with relish.

On the walk home I tried unsuccessfully to engage her in conversation. Finally, in exasperation, I asked,

"What's eating you, Kate? Can I help?"

She looked at her feet as we continued walking and shook her head. "No one can help."

I didn't know how to respond to that. My own swirling emotions were crowding out words.

"So what are you going to do?"

"Nothing I can do," and after a pause—"except kill myself, that's all."

We walked along in the dusk of early evening, each of us locked in our own dark thoughts. Kate broke the silence.

"What hope is there for me—coming from where I do? Genes can't be changed, my tough luck."

"Mary inherited the same genes; she seems to be getting along all right with them," I replied.

"My sister!" Kate interrupted with contempt. "All she knows is her husband and now the baby. She has no expectations, no aspirations. She's happy—happy like a stupid cow."

"You told me yourself that Mary and her husband were kind to you. What do you expect of them anyhow?" I wanted to know.

"Nothing, that's exactly it. Nothing, and she doesn't recognize that is what she has, nothing. Don't you understand?"

No, I didn't, but I remained silent. I left Kate that evening with my thoughts in turmoil. I checked with Mary daily. After another week had passed with no sign that Kate's depression would lift, Mary called a psychiatrist to the house. As a result of his visit, Kate agreed to enter a psychiatric hospital for treatment. I visited her there and she talked with me freely. She described the shock treatment she had undergone and vowed that she would never again submit to it. She pointed out patients she had met whose tragic stories she had learned. It occurred to me that she was exchanging her personal depression for the burden of the collective mental miseries of all the other patients.

My second visit found her much improved and after a month or two she was released and was able to resume her job and some of her activities.

It was at about this period of her recovery that I moved to Los Angeles. Our correspondence was rather erratic so I was not concerned when I did not hear from her for some time. In correspondence with a mutual friend, however, I learned that Kate had had a serious relapse and had committed herself to the state hospital just outside Philadelphia.

I returned to Philadelphia for a visit perhaps a half year after Kate's commitment and found she was still an inmate at the hospital. I went to see her there and she was delighted to see me, as I was to see her. She looked alive, relaxed, and I couldn't help wondering why she lingered in that place. As she talked it became clear that while she was much improved, her treatment was not yet complete. She told me proudly that she had un-restricted movement within the facility and that as part of her therapy she worked as secretary to one of the staff doctors. She looked forward to her work and was daily growing in confidence. When it was time for me to leave she walked me to the outside gate and said, "This is as far as I can go today but it won't be long now before I'll be walking through that gate for good."

Many years passed before I saw Kate again on one of my periodic visits to Philadelphia. We met in town for dinner and I had an eerie feeling that what I knew had happened in the interim had really not happened. Except for furrows that had deepened on her forehead and the fact that the red hair of her youth had turned a darker, more sedate shade, she was the same Kate I had known in the old days. She was warm, interested, friendly, yet reserved. She told me she was working, that she lived in an apartment in an old brownstone in town and, finally and shyly, she added that she was sharing the apartment with a friend, a man. Would I care to walk over to her apartment and meet him? He probably would be at home.

On the way she related that her friend had also had a mental breakdown in early life and was presently going through a painful divorce. She had reservations about marrying him and, in effect, merging their problems. "But," she said, "we'll see. Meanwhile, we're together and that's enough for now."

I remembered to ask after her sister. "Oh, I see Mary now and then," Kate said. "I never went back to live with her, though. She knows that I will always be grateful that she stuck with me through my illness. She knows, too, that we are too different to ever be close in spite of the unhappy childhood we shared." That is the last time I saw Kate. I left her with a good feeling. She seemed on the brink of a lasting happiness. And yet there was a fragility about her, a vulnerability that I fear could bring her low again. What if she foundered once again? Could she rise up, or would she wither and the light go out?

How often I've thought of Kate in the intervening years. What is it that keeps me from seeking her out and rekindling our friendship? Is it simply the passage of years? I no longer have an address for her—true. True also that she was the one who had stopped writing. So what!

It wouldn't be that hard to find her. Just a few short years ago one of my Philadelphia friends mentioned that she had run into Kate in town. She went on to say that Kate looked "weird" and that she was dressed "funny." Her hair, once so lovely, hung about her face with no attempt at styling. Kate had shown no inclination to prolong the conversation beyond the polite exchange of greetings.

I didn't want to hear that, and I remember that I had asked no further questions. Nevertheless, the questions are there and Kate keeps popping into my mind at odd times, uninvited, yet not to be ignored. I really must look her up and resolve the unknown. It will be all right, I tell myself, if I encounter a new, a different Kate so long as she is whole and at peace with herself. The dread is that I may find a defeated Kate, a Kate disintegrated and beyond mending, a lost soul.

I cannot have an old friend be left dangling, ghostlike, in my consciousness. I must find her and re-establish her reality, no matter what that might finally prove to be. I will find her, and hope she will let me be her friend.

SELECTION ELEVEN

YOU CAN'T ALWAYS
GO HOME AGAIN

by Selma Lewin

THIS IS LOS ANGELES ON A WARM SUMMER evening. I have lived at this general location, in this once highly desirable upper-middle-class Wilshire area, for many years. Forty, as a matter of fact. I am astonished to realize how much time has passed, how firmly circumstances have planted me here, and how things have changed. I have been an owner, then a tenant and now manager.

It is a congested, predominantly Latino neighborhood, and on this balmy evening people are in good spirits, ebullient and jolly, because it's Friday night and the first of the month; it's payday and Social Security and welfare checks and food stamps. Though most people here work very hard at low-paying jobs, many are illegal aliens and work on the "QT."

There is much laughing and calling out to one another. The man next door thrusts his head back and guffaws in response to some funny remark hollered out from a window. Everyone laughs. There is no way I can join in the fun. I am a foreigner in my own country.

Children are playing ball on the sidewalk, good old American ball, but they are playing in Spanish. The kids will not be called into bed until eleven, twelve o'clock at night. Whoever has remained indoors is blasting radio and TV in Spanish, at unendurable decibels.

In the building next door there are thirty-two apartments, singles, and if each single housed one occupant there would be thirty-two people. But although these apartments consist of one large room, kitchenette and bath, the usual occupants are two adults and two or three kids, even three kids and an infant on the way. So you have possibly 150 souls, a little community by itself in this one building next door.

They haven't much, but always plenty to throw away. On Wednesdays the boulevard is lined with old chairs and sofas with escaping stuffing, broken TV's, burned skillets, etc. The avenue of discarded mattresses.

Many have broken down (very broken down) cars and no garages. This causes conflict with my tenants who can't get out of our driveway due to illegal parking. They are always polite. "I'm sorry," they say after much blasting of horns from our tenants. It's a big, ongoing problem. The block is just too crowded, especially the big apartments like the building next door. How do they manage? How do they conduct their conjugal life? This always puzzles me. But that they do is patently apparent; so many smiling young mothers-to-be. Some so young they look about fifteen. Babies having babies.

The kids are cute, out playing like all kids, but they play in Spanish. I don't understand, don't they go to school? One young mother who speaks some English told me she speaks only Spanish to her children because she does not want them to lose their culture. What about my culture? Will I lose it? What will really resolve the bilingual question?

The children are sweet but uncharming when they answer nature's call right on the sidewalk. "Hey," I said to a seven-year-old, "Why don't you go upstairs? Or at least behind a bush?" "It's a free country," he told me. True. There was something uplifting about his having caught the American spirit. A free country. I tried to explain that freedom must be protected, at least to the extent of making wee-wee indoors, using the facilities provided for such an emergency. And not just the kids. I have seen grown men commit this transgression not too discreetly and, most puzzling of all, just after having come out of a building.

Part of the culture? Overcrowding, poverty, disenfranchised, ethnic? It is easy to see why countries have problems with ethnic diversity; ethnic diversity doesn't go down that well in our own country.

Odd, illegal businesses spring up overnight. A panel truck is parked illegally on the lawn festooned with clothing, blouses, shirts and skirts. Little girls' party dresses, pink and lacy. A hand-painted sign says, "Ropas Baratos," and, in concession to a non-Latino buyer, "Close Cheep."

Another business couple have stacked pillows on the grocery lot, against the wall under the graffiti. A tenant in one of the buildings has decided to market her homemade tamales. She sits on the stoop besides her large cauldron of tamales, wearing an apron with a big pocket for change, and hawks to the passer-by, "Tamales! Tamales!"

A group of people are sitting on my lawn, as if it were a park, eating tamales. They do not live here. And where will they leave the wrappers? Am I a misanthrope to be disturbed by this? But where *shall* they sit? Many of the buildings where they live are flush with the street; there is no lawn. I try to be understanding.

A teenager toots his horn loud and long, summoning a friend. Horn blowing is a major problem here. Most do not have phones, and no place to park results in a lot of nerve-wracking horn blowing all hours of day and night. I ask this young fellow to tone it down. Most of the young people are polite and respectful but this one answers with a four letter Anglo-Saxon expletive. "Oh," I say, "I see you are learning English."

A woman walks by, hands swinging at her sides, carrying a large bundle on top of her head. It does not impede her stride. Amazing. "Tamales! Tamales!" It goes on.

A bazaar, Mardi Gras atmosphere, exotic and lively. But I am lonely. With my limited Spanish and my own cultural background there is not much communication. It is as though I have been on a vacation to Mexico and now I want to go home. And once again I must remind myself—I am home. This is home?

SELECTION TWELVE

THE *ANSCHLUSS* OF AUSTRIA
by Edith Ehrenreich

T HE FIRST TWELVE YEARS OF MY LIFE I LIVE IN Vienna, the city where I was born. To me it seems the greatest and most beautiful city in the world. When I am about eight or ten years old, I invent a detective game. My friend and I play it whenever we have time. This is the way it works: we stand behind an apartment-house door and we count to ten. Then we step out onto the street, and the first person who passes us, we trail wherever they go. The game is to follow them without them noticing us. We spend hours following people from one end of the city to the other. Nobody ever notices us. Soon we know the city inside out. I love that game, because I love the old streets, the old houses. I like the atmosphere.

My parents and I live in a rather small and dingy apartment. Few people own their own house, or even a car, so the streets are filled with people walking, catching streetcars, shopping; the streets are busy with hustle and bustle.

I like the city; but I learn soon that I don't really belong—I am considered different.

One day in 1934, my mother and I are going through the inner part of the city, close to the Ring. Suddenly we hear shots nearby. People are running in all directions. No one seems to know what has happened. Later that day we find out that the Prime Minister has been assassinated. The government has now been taken over by the Christian Republicans. The first thing they do that affects me is to introduce prayers in the schools. Now I and the other children in my class begin to realize that some of us are different.

There are four Jewish children in my class of about thirty-five. We do not participate in the morning prayers. I realize that we are the objects of both envy and resentment. One schoolmate says to me, "How come you don't have to do this? Don't you believe in Christ?" Well, then the whole business of religion is dredged up, and soon some of our classmates call us Christ-killers and other fine names.

My friend Ilse and I are walking to school. We have been schoolmates since the first grade. Since September we have been in the 5th grade, attending a new private school for girls. It is April 1938.

We are going the same way as usual. It is a sunny April morning, kind of breezy. We walk pretty fast. We will get into trouble if we are late. Finally we come to this huge, heavy wooden door in a tall stone building. It is always hard to open this door. We come in, and we are surprised how quiet it is. Nobody is downstairs. Maybe we are late and classes have started. We look up the staircase, and on the second floor, along the banister, a lot of girls are standing. I recognize some of my classmates. They are looking at us. Under the banister is a big sign made of white butcher paper. In large capital letters the sign says: "PIGS AND JEWS ARE NOT ALLOWED TO ENTER HERE."

Then it becomes very noisy. Everybody is shouting and laughing, and throwing stuff: erasers, crayons, notebooks, balled-up papers. It is like a birthday party in reverse. Ilse and I stand there for a while. It seems a long time. We look at each other. We run down the street. We slow down and cross an open area in an out-door market. A man comes toward us. When he is about ten feet away from us, he says: "Jew dogs!" And then he spits.

Ilse and I continue walking. We come to the park by our house. We are very warm now and out of breath. We run to a bench. The bench has chalk writing on it: "For Aryans only." We look for a bench without any writing. Only one bench has a sign in red paint: "For filthy Jews only."

This was the day after the *anschluss* (annexation) of Austria to Germany in 1938. Ilse and I walk back to our own homes. We are scared. We know life will not be the same again.

After Austria is annexed and becomes a Nazi state, my life changes considerably. I attend no school for a while, until a school for "Jews only" opens up. We are evicted from our apartment, and rent a room from another Jewish family, who is also in the process of being evicted. So we move from one family and one room to another. My father was employed in a synagogue. Now he has no job because the Temple was set on fire and burned down.

My father takes me to visit my grandfather in Czechoslovakia for the first time. I'm looking forward to the visit. He is the only grandparent I have who is still alive.

Grandfather lives in a small village. He meets us in front of his house in the courtyard. I expect a hug and a smile. Instead, he places his hand in front of my face and asks me to kiss it. I'm shocked. I never had to do this before. I don't like it.

During my few weeks stay at his house, there are a number of things he does that I really dislike. He corrects everything I do. I don't fold the tablecloth the right way; I don't know the prayers well enough; my manners need to improve.

One day, when my step-grandmother prepares my most favorite dish, he takes a huge portion for himself, but doles out a most skinny little helping for me.

I find myself trying to stay out of his way. I am disappointed in him. I am glad to leave when my father comes to pick me up. I have no wish to visit him again. There is little love lost between us.

My father gets arrested. We think we will never get to see him again. By some miracle he gets released because of his Czech citizenship. We know it is only a matter of time now, and that next time we may not be saved. The wait seems endless. Every knock on the door makes our heartbeat stop.

And then, one day in August 1939, the long awaited permit to emigrate finally comes in the mail. It feels exactly like a reprieve from a death sentence.

In September, on the eve of Yom Kippur, our Day of Atonement, we are actually on the train that is going to lead us out of this hell. On this train are other Jewish people. I make friends with one of the girls my age. We travel throughout the night, but no one sleeps. The men say the prayers appropriate for the Holiday. There is such a feeling of hope and gratitude in all of us.

Morning time comes. We have finally come to the last station which is in the city of Cologne, the border town between Germany and Holland. Everyone gets off and turns in their passports to the Station Master for inspection. There are about 60 people all together. We drag off our belongings. My parents and I sit among the others, waiting to be called to board the shuttle train which will lead us into Holland. No one is eating. The Day of Atonement is a fast day. We don't even feel hungry. We just talk to each other in quiet voices.

Soon the names are called. One by one, each family boards the shuttle train that will take them across the border to Holland. Our friends are called. We just wave to them, knowing we'll see them soon on the train. Pretty soon everyone's name has been called except ours. To our horror, we see the train pulling away from the station. My parents run over to the Station Master. They can't believe that this is happening to us. He shakes his head. We are not allowed to cross the border. He says, "You are Czech citizens and Czechoslovakia is considered an enemy country."

I look at my parents. There is no color in their faces. They are standing speechless. A policeman, very tall and well-built, comes to take us to the police station. Then we know that our death sentence has not been commuted. My whole body starts to shake. My father lifts the heavy trunks. My mother and I carry a smaller suitcase, but it feels as if it contains lead. We walk a long distance through the city streets. My father stops every once in a while to catch his breath. The sweat is pouring down his face. My mother tries to pick up the trunks and wants to carry them a few steps, but my father grabs them away from her. The policeman keeps prodding him along. People stare at us. I hear them saying, "Look at the Jews!" I hold my head as high as I can. I don't look at anyone.

After a long time we arrive at the police station. We are told to sit and wait until the police chief comes. We sit on a wooden bench. I sit next to my father. My mother is on the other side of him. I cannot see her face. I don't want to look at her.

It is a well-lit, roomy place. It is Sunday morning. We are told that the police chief is not at the station yet. We sit in absolute silence. I look only at the door. I keep thinking: "We should run away as fast as we can. Why are we sitting here?" I look at my father's face for a moment. I see tears running down. I have never seen my father cry before. I feel like vomiting.

Occasionally the phone rings. There are no other sounds in the place. I don't know how long we sit there. A policeman finally comes out of the office. We have not seen him before. He tells us that the police chief is still at home, but that he will call him to find out what to do with us. Now we all know: the answer means life or death. I keep thinking, "We have no power at all. It all depends on one man who doesn't even know us, whether we live or die. Why should anyone have this right?"

Then the door to the office opens again. I don't look up. I am not breathing. The policeman says to my father: "The police chief said to let the Jews go." We stand up. My father puts his arms around me and my mother. He is sobbing. I think, "If I were God I would destroy the whole country this moment."

After our reprieve from the police chief, I hardly remember our way back to the train station. But we carry all our stuff back. It seems a lot lighter. A shuttle train is provided for us, and we are the only passengers on board. It is about a five minute ride across the border. It is early afternoon. The sun is shining directly through the train window. It is bright.

Soon we are at the train depot in Holland. The three of us get out. We look and smell like a most bedraggled bunch. We have not slept for thirty-six hours, we have not eaten or taken a sip of liquid for an equal amount of time, and we have just experienced one of the most traumatic events of our lives. The sweat is still pouring from us; our tear-stained faces and our wrinkled clothes are a sight to behold.

The Dutch train looks more like the inside of a streetcar. When I get on, I notice that some benches are facing the door. The rest of the seats face the direction in which the train is going. All seats are occupied.

As soon as my parents and I get on, three or four

people jump up from the bench facing the door. I am sure that they can't stand the sight of us and want to get away. But, No! They grab our belongings and stack them in the overhead luggage compartment. Then they come toward us and ask us to take their seats. My father, who never wants to accept anything from anybody, shakes his head. But they take him firmly by the arm and seat him on the bench. Someone, I can't remember who, gently leads me to a seat next to my parents. One lady, who speaks excellent German, asks us if we are refugees. All we say is: "Yes!" Within minutes half a dozen people come over to us and bring us all kinds of food. Coffee and bread with cheese for my parents. I get hot chocolate, a box of candy, and an apple. We sit there in absolute astonishment. For about a year and a half we have been in constant fear of our neighbors, even our so-called friends. And now these perfect strangers treat us as if we were their long-lost family.

Several of the people on the train talk to my parents about conditions in Germany. They ask many questions.

When we arrive in Rotterdam, one of the Dutch people calls the Jewish Agency for us and waits with us until we are picked up and taken care of.

We stay for six weeks in Holland until we are able to board the ship which brings us to America. Those are the best weeks of my youth.

To this day, whenever someone tells me that they are Dutch, I feel related to them.

I never saw my grandfather again. He was exterminated along with millions of other European Jews before I had a chance to forgive him for his petty idiosyncrasies, and ask his forgiveness for my own lack of love and respect. To this day, whenever I think of him, I feel a deep sense of guilt.

SELECTION THIRTEEN

FESSEX, FESSEX, PRENEZ GARDE!

Isidore Ziferstein

THE TWO SAMMYS (MY COUSIN SAMMY YAGOLNIT-
zer and my schoolmate and friend Sam Rosenberg)
and I are now at the age when we do a lot of girl-watch-
ing from a safe distance. We not only watch, we also
drool.

But alas! not one of the girls we drool over even
gives us a second look. We're convinced that the three of
us are doomed to eternal bachelorhood. We talk a lot
about this. We talk a lot about girls. After much
deliberation, we arrive at the unanimous conclusion
that all girls are by nature hard-hearted and cruel, that
girls take a perverse pleasure in looking infinitely ap-
pealing, and then teasing and depriving the likes of us.

The only logical antidote to being forever lovesick
and frustrated is: strike back at the monsters! Show
them our contempt! Show them that our hearts are
pure; that we are above and beyond temptation by those

wanton frails. We are, and shall always be, committed and sworn woman-haters.

The three of us form an exclusive, secret club, with a constitution and byelaws. The name of our threesome shall be "The Anti-Fessex League." (Fessex is our patented top-secret code-word for the fair sex.)

Our Constitution begins with the immortal words of the Declaration of Independence: "When in the course of human events it becomes necessary for one gender to dissolve the bonds which have enslaved it to the other gender, and to assume the separate and equal station to which the Laws of Nature and of Nature's God entitle it..." Our Constitution then proceeds with appropriately modified excerpts from the Preamble to the Constitution of the United States, the Emancipation Proclamation, and Lincoln's Gettysburg Address, and ends with the ringing declaration that "We mutually pledge our Lives, our Fortunes, and our sacred Honor to the cause of freeing the males of this world from the yoke of enslavement by the so-called Fair Sex."

The byelaws require and pledge each of us, whenever and wheresoever we encounter a female of the opposite sex, to throw down the gauntlet, and challenge her with our battle-cry, "Fessex, Fessex, Prenez Garde!"

Not long after the formation of the Anti-Fessex League, I am invited by my friend Meyer Rosenbaum to his younger sister Bella's Sweet Sixteen party. I have been secretly in love with Bella for years. She looks adorable in her King Tut haircut—short, with its crescent curve and points jutting out over her cheeks at the bottom of the crescent. For years I have hoped that Bella would reciprocate my deep abiding, though unspoken, true love. But she, cruel dame, knows nothing of my love. She goes out with older "men," who have steady jobs and coins jingling in their pockets. Just like a woman, she has chosen money over true love. I hate her for being so profligate and mercenary.

However, at the mere mention of Bella's name, my heart melts. In flagrant violation of my vows to the Anti-Fessex League, I had written a long poem, in emulation of John Milton's "L'Allegro." It begins with the following verse:

> "Bella, oh beautiful Bella!
> Thy name doth thee not justice.
> For in heaven thou art yclept Bellissima."

And now I'll be a guest at Bella's party. Oh, joy! I accept Meyer's invitation a little too eagerly. My eagerness could betray my long-kept secret to Meyer. But Meyer doesn't notice. I ask Meyer airily,

"Is it OK if I bring a friend, a boy, that is, to the party?"

"Sure, it's OK," says Meyer, "Bella has invited all her girlfriends and she's worried that there won't be enough boys."

Too many girls?! Not enough boys?! Oh, glory! Ah, bliss! I'll invite my fellow woman-hater Sam Rosenberg to join me in sin.

Sam accepts my invitation to help fill the gender gap at Bella's party. But he says, "Izzy, I'm just doing this as a favor to you. I remain true to the cause of woman-hating, and I hope you will too."

The party is well-attended. Boys and girls overflow all the rooms of the Rosenbaum railroad flat. There are awkward introductions. The girls blush and giggle a lot.

These lovable, timid blushers and gigglers, are they the dangerous creatures against whom we have sworn a vendetta?!

The introductions are followed by dancing to the music of the Rosenbaum's brand new player-piano. I manage to get a dance with Bella. I am overjoyed. Bellissima is in my arms! I am so excited that my feet don't follow the rhythm of the player-piano music. I all but step all over Bella's feet.

After these preliminaries, we settle down to the serious business of the party—kissing games: "Spin the Bottle," "Post Office," "Wink," and more. I get to kiss almost all the girls. And I discover that I do not hate them at all. I love every one of them. They are so lovely, and tender, and so soft to the touch!

Carried away by all the dancing, and hugging, and kissing, I have all but forgotten about my friend, my comrade-in-arms and fellow woman-hater, Sam Rosenberg. The last time I saw him, he had been standing in a corner of the room glaring angrily at me and at the girls I was so ingloriously kissing. Why isn't Sam joining in the fun? Could it be because he is two years younger than I, and at fourteen he is not old enough to appreciate the ecstasy of kissing games?

Now Sam strides over to where I'm sitting in the circle of revellers, grabs my shoulder, and hisses, "Izzy, I wanna talk to you, right now!" I follow him obediently into the corridor. Sam is now shouting, "Izzy, I'm ashamed of you, and disgusted. How can you so degrade yourself! I'm leaving this house of ill-fame right now, and you're coming with me."

I'm torn between my loyalty to Sam and my new-found love for all sixteen-year-old girls in the world. Sam stalks out of the house. He expects me to be strong, and to follow him. But, alas, I am weak. I return to the festivities in the Rosenbaum's front room.

And so begins my fall from grace. No sooner am I confronted with the first temptation than, through weakness of character, combined with the power of the raging juices, I break the faith. I become helplessly and hopelessly bewitched by girlkind. I am a traitor to the cause of Anti-Fessex.

SELECTION FOURTEEN

FIRST DAYS
by E.S.

I DIED ON JULY 9TH, 1984, IN LOS ANGELES, AFTER a brief illness. I do not remember much pain, although the violence of the infection that caused my death must have brought acute discomfort and consuming fever. I do remember, though, when I knew I would not live. My doctor had given me an injection and I felt suddenly pure and without substance. More than that, I saw my room, a nurse, my doctor, from an angle not at all relative to the position of my bed. They seemed farther away and lower, as if I myself were slightly levitated. Then I saw myself, one arm dangling over the edge of my bed and Janet, my wife, holding my hand. She was sitting on a chair, bent toward me.

It was confusing, for although I seemed above and out of myself, I could still feel the warmth of Janet's hand and see the look in her eye. I must have been like an image split in two when one's eyes, fixed on it, are out of focus...a candle flame that becomes two identical flames. Like a faint voice on a telephone, Janet's voice

was saying, "You're doing fine, Ed. You're doing fine..."
She looked gray with fatigue, and her mouth, usually so
pliant, seemed to have difficulty forming the words; but
her eyes were the reflection of my own knowledge. They
said, "He is dying."

I could not speak, but I matched the dishonesty of
her words by smiling. It must have been a poor smile,
because Janet's head sagged on my arm and the nurse
turned her face away.

Then it happened. I remember one final spasm.
And, I remember thinking to myself, this must be the
delivery of my soul; and I saw then a primitive Italian
painting in reds and blues, where, from the prostrate
body of a noble lord, escapes the white smoke of his
spirit, freed. But there was this strange addiction: I was
for the time both the bearer and the born, the issuant
and the issue. I was at the same moment creating and
being created, and I could not tell which was the more
difficult—the black fighting up into the light, or the
more familiar expulsion of my burden.

But that is only part of the story. So much happened in what must have been so short a time that any
ordered description is misleading. And yet the only way
I can convey the simultaneous rush of sensations is to
tell each of them one after the other, although they are
no more separate than the separate colors that go to
make up white. And I shall have to use the world's arbitrary measurements of time—days, weeks, months—
to parcel out this chronicle of space.

First, with a fearful roar and clanging, as if a thousand metal hearts were beating against their walls, I
was whirled into an emptiness as crowded with substance as are certain silences with sound. It was a wild
and headlong flight, where I spun and reeled and pal-
pitated like a leaf in a hurricane. In all this roaring and
palpitating there was music...voices, phrases, instru-
ments engaged in some gigantic prelude (to what sym-

phony?). And there were words: fragments of poems; and through them all I, myself, screaming (to whom?) "Hold me!"—for the loneliness was terrible.

And Janet held me. Rather, she held a shell, for I had slipped out of it, as a hand from a glove. My body lay there, completely still. But it had no more to do with me than the starched white cap of the nurse who went to Janet and gently tried to pull back her shoulders. Janet raised her head slowly and looked with blind eyes toward the door. My doctor, standing there, moved toward her.

The headlong rush, the wheeling and roaring, stopped and a great silence came. I seemed to be quivering like a seismographic needle suspended in a stationary dance. This took place in an electric and impalpable void that had no boundaries. The nearest visual quality of this void is the queer light that one can see when the eyes are tightly shut against the sun. I was not alone. In this featureless state, there was a definite pattern of which I seemed to be only one point of many. This, presumably, was the final breakdown of matter.

A great peace settled over me. I had not realized until this moment how heavy was the burden of identity. This is the end, thank God, of Edward Scott; the end of this terrible and vigilant consciousness...the end of doubt, of pain, of error; the end, even, of emotion; and the beginning of freedom.

As usual, I was a fool.

◊ ◊ ◊

I should not have been surprised, therefore, to find myself present at my funeral. The few times Janet and I talked of death, I'd raged against funerals. "For heaven's sake, don't give me one if I die. I think funerals are barbaric and miserable; it's destructive to true memory."

Janet laughed at me as if I were a willful child.

"Okay, dear—we'll just dump you into the nearest ditch!"

I was dumped, instead, into a non-denominational church at Forest Lawn, in a very elaborate casket. The church was crowded, which surprised me. Janet, Jon, and Victoria were in the first pew, of course. Behind them were assorted cousins, aunts and uncles; Janet's brother and sister and their children; Emma, our cook of so many years. I recognized many friends, but there were many more I did not recognize. In the back pew of the chapel sat Laura. There were shadows under her eyes and she seemed very, very tired.

The altar was covered with flowers. At the right of it, the organist waited at the keyboard, his head turned to watch the cortege. At a signal from the head usher, the organ began to play the choral prelude, *Ich Ruf Zu Dir*. Jon must have arranged that, for we heard it together when he was thirteen, and at the end I had asked what he thought of it. After a pause he had said, "I guess that's religion." I told him it was mine; then added, half to myself, "I'd like to die listening to it."

The pallbearers were carrying my coffin slowly up the aisle. Laura did not look at the coffin. Neither did Jon. The boy was fixing his eyes, enlarged but dry, on an organ pipe. The only movement I could see was his collar working up and down on his thin neck. His hands were closed so tightly into fists, hanging at his sides, that the knuckles were white. His inaudible voice kept saying, over and over, "This Isn't Dad, This Isn't Dad."

Janet, correct and grave, followed the cortege with her eyes, and so did Victoria. Mourning became my wife; it refined her face and gave her bearing dignity. I think she was too tired to feel much, except a kind of incredulity. Over and over, she said, "My Husband Is Dead. My Husband Is Dead"—as if to convince herself of something she doubted. As for Victoria, my daughter, her stepdaughter, tears were streaming down her face.

But they were not tears of uncontrollable grief. As clearly as if she were speaking above the crowd in her girl's voice, the words came out: "I Have No Father. He Was Famous And Everybody Is Here And Looking At Me. I Look Like Him. I Am All In Black And Very Pale And Everybody Is Saying, 'Poor Child, How Like Her Father.'" All that Laura whispered was, "Stay with me."

I suppose, in spite of my aversion to funerals, mine could have been called a simple and unpretentious one. With few exceptions, these people had come to grieve for and honor me; with few exceptions, they loved me in their own separate ways. The dissonant notes (and I heard them as clearly as if the organist had struck them) came from two others besides Victoria, my daughter. There was Janet's sister, Julie, whose abiding reaction was, "Thank God Janet's Free Of That Man." And there was Elly, my cousin, who considered my early death as a sort of fitting answer to what she had always believed was an amoral and indulgent life. When the three of them got together in the vestibule after the service was over, muttering to each other about the "Tragic Loss," it was a wonder that a gigantic projection of my smile did not alarm them into silence.

I must explain that this extra-terrestrial eavesdropping of mine was accompanied by a complete absence of emotion. As far as I can see, this was a sort of compensation for total vision, which in life would have been unbearable. It was as though I were looking down at a borderless oriental rug of infinitely complex design. I could see each part in relation to every other part. I could see the deer stepping through the flowers and, at the same time, the man raising his bow to shoot at it. I could see the arrow speed and the deer stricken. I could see the river winding among the hills and the women drinking at its source. I could see two men fighting and one of them dead. The light was the same all over; nothing was in shadow.

There was, of course, no element of time. Or rather, past, present, and future co-existed exactly as they do in the world "today." In these early stages of seeing without feeling, I thought to myself, "This is Heaven." Later on I said, "This is Hell."

Will had died with my body. I was totally at the beck and call of those who remembered, needed, and wanted me. They re-created me in their own wills, they conjured up my presence, they plucked me out of my crowded electric void and gave me shape, if not substance. And, how long this slavery to the living (for that is what it was) would last, I could not tell. I was often in three or four places at once, especially in the weeks immediately following my death. The continuity of this record is, therefore, an arbitrary one.

I was a fool to think that any such drastic transition could be completed all at once, any more than an adolescent can become wholly mature overnight. Like every growth, it was a slow process. And it was to be a long time before I could really leave my life, before the severance from the world I knew was final.

◊ ◊ ◊

Now you have arrived at the end of this small journey. You have absorbed the techniques of writing from within, of writing in an authentic voice. You have reflected on the experiences and stages of your life, worked on your stories, and read a number of other stories which may have served as models for your own writing and rewriting. In the course of working with this volume, you have explored your own creativity—your ability to re-express what you have seen and felt in life—and have experienced the pleasure of writing well.

Perhaps you have also come to view the difficulties you've encountered in your life in a new light, gaining a new understanding of their meaning and a new respect for the ways in which you handled yourself in the circumstances. In the course of writing your life's stories you may also have given a great deal of pleasure to and provoked considerable thought and feeling in your readers and listeners. If this is so, then keep writing, and encourage those you love to do the same.

Appendix

Developing
Supportive Feedback

A KEY ASPECT OF SUCCEEDING AS A WRITER IS knowing when and where to get guidance, support, and assistance. As writers, most of us need feedback from others. Whether it comes from members of a writers' group, an editor, or some other trusted source, feedback is important. In this Appendix, I will suggest ways of getting positive support and feedback, and will tell you how to get the most out of it in order to continue to grow in your work.

We have all encountered criticism from different people during our lives. We probably remember how stung we felt when teachers, parents, and even friends criticized us when we were doing the best we could. Such criticism felt particularly harsh when we were doing something artistic—writing, painting, drawing, or playing a musical instrument. Often, we simply stopped doing these artistic things. Gradually, we internalized this criticism and developed our own inner critic.

Now that we are going to do some writing, we need to retrain this inner critic. Otherwise, we may not go on writing after the first bit of harsh criticism we receive when we share our work with others—and we *do need* feedback.

Retraining one's inner critic is no small or easy task. It can be accomplished, however, by patience, discipline, and a positive outlook. The same process can also be used to retrain the critic within members of your support structure, or your students. First, let us consider the kind of feedback we as writers would *like* to experience. Then I will outline a process by which the wild, undisciplined, even destructive critic within yourself can be converted to a purposeful, disciplined, insightful one.

SUPPORTIVE FEEDBACK: WHAT IS IT?

A group, or even one like-minded person, can help you get the kind of feedback you need. This person or group to whom you are going to turn for support needs to develop a disciplined response to your writing, to protect you and make you feel safe while guiding you in the direction of better work. That discipline involves adhering strictly to the following agreement which each participant will make with other participants: feedback to each writer after he or she shares a story will be Non-Judgmental, Non-Invasive, Corrective, and Affirming (NJNICA, for short). Each person giving feedback agrees to avoid any statement that sounds judgmental or invasive no matter how innocently he or she intends it. During the early sessions of any group one person may be appointed to be on the lookout for such judgmental and invasive statements.

A. Typical judgmental statements are:

1. You *should* have....

2. You *could* have....

3. You *ought* to have....

4. That (story, thought, paragraph, etc.) was *too* (sentimental, clever, abrupt, silly, slow, confusing, boring, etc.)

B. Typical invasive questions and statements are:

1. Why did (or didn't) you...?

2. Why were you...?

3. You sound like you were angry with your... and were trying....

4. You often... or always....

Any one of these statements directed at a writer can discourage him or her. Instead, ask members of your group to try

A. Non-judgmental corrective statements such as:

1. I would like to (see, feel, be able to follow, etc.)

2. I had trouble seeing the picture.

3. I had difficulty following the action.

4. I needed to feel the character's feelings.

5. I found my attention wandering.

6. I needed to hear the characters talk to each other more.

7. I had difficulty finding (or following) the spine of the story.

8. I didn't know what question I was supposed to ask in the beginning.

9. I didn't know what the central question of the story was.

10. The key question was answered for me before I had a chance to get involved or get excited about it.

B. Non-judgmental affirming statements such as:

1. I saw the picture clearly.

2. I was right there with you the whole time.

3. I knew what each character (or the narrator) was feeling from one moment to the next.

4. The dialogue drew me in and helped me know each character.

5. The balance of narrative, dialogue and inner thoughts and feelings held my interest.

These are important considerations. A potential writer can listen all day and be helped by non-judgmental, non-invasive, corrective, and affirming (NJNICA) comments. He can listen for only a few moments to invasive or judgmental statements. Then he will begin to defend himself, his creativity will turn off, and he will stop writing.

You may find that your support system is only one person, or perhaps you and a friend decide to write your life stories and share them. One person is enough if his or her feedback is non-invasive, non-judgmental, corrective, and affirming.

The great advantage of working in a group or with a trusted friend is that the writer can stop being the critic and simply create. Each person can then be a responsible critic for the other writers when they read their stories. So keep looking for one or two people with whom you can share this very special journey of self-exploration.

However, if the person you select to review your work simply says, "I like it," or "I don't like it," and shows no inclination to go beyond such statements, get a new partner. Liking or not liking is superficial and not helpful. Likewise, if he or she gives you judgmental or invasive comments, find someone who is willing to provide NJNICA feedback. If you find yourself alone and unable to develop a writer-reviewer relationship with anyone, then you need to develop these NJNICA qualities in yourself.

If you are a teacher and you wish to encourage your students to write their life stories, it is important to develop habits of NJNICA feedback in them.

The six exercises below will help you develop NJNICA feedback, and may be tried alone or in a group.

1. Review each of the following stories contained in this book.

   A. Willem (1) (p. 21)

   B. Goose Story (1) (p. 58)

   C. The Typhoon of Forty-Five — First Draft (p. 161)

2. Appoint one person to roleplay the "writer" of each story. If you are that writer, you may *defend* what has been written any time you feel that the criticism voiced at you is hostile, judgmental, invasive, or superficial. When the critique of "your" work is over, tell the others what it felt like: who was achieving NJNICA feedback and who was not.

3. If you are giving the writer feedback, describe your responses to the story aloud. If you are doing this alone, talk into a tape recorder, or speak aloud, or, as a last resort, write it down.

Focus your attention on how you responded to the story rather than on how the story is written (i.e., "I needed more detail," "I found my attention wandering," etc., rather than "It's too long, too confusing," etc.).

If the person roleplaying the writer begins to defend himself, it is a clue that you or others in the group are being judgmental or invasive or superficial. Find a NJNICA comment that will make the point.

By giving NJNICA feedback which focuses on your reactions to the story, you leave the writer room to make choices about what to change and what not to change.

Have each person in the group defend or absorb feedback for five minutes. Continue until each person in the group has had a chance to roleplay the writer. The comments may be repetitive, but the purpose of the task is to experience (1) being a writer under the gun, and (2) changing your mode of giving feedback from judgmental or superficial to NJNICA.

4. In each story, address the following issues:

A. Willem (1)

—Is the point of view child or adult?

—Is the story written in the present or as a recollection?

—Is the level of language child or adult?

—Is the situation believable?

—Are the writer's feelings clearly expressed?

B. Goose Story (1)

—Is the picture clear?

—Are the writer's feelings clearly expressed?

—Where should the dialogue begin?

—Where should the "setting the stage" material go?

C. The Typhoon of Forty-Five — First Draft

—Is the picture clear?

—Are the writer's feelings clearly expressed?

—Do we need more details? What kind?

—Do we need more dialogue? What kind?

—Do we get the feelings of the narrator moment to moment?

—What is the meaning of the story?

5. When the initial critique of each story is complete, read the final version of the story aloud, again appointing a writer to defend or explain the work. Remember, there are no *right* answers to the issues. We are attending to the task of creating feedback and promoting lively discussions.

Give yourself and your friend or group at least one session per story, perhaps one or two sessions a week.

6. After the third session you will be ready for feedback on your own stories. If you have not written you earliest memories yet, read the first two

chapters in the book, then follow the steps below if you have one or more persons giving feedback.

A. Tell your earliest memory aloud into a tape recorder or to your friend or group. Get a few NJNICA comments, then retell the story in the present tense "I am five years old and I am..." rather than "I was...."

B. Write your story just as you have told it aloud. If the group is large or time is running short, do the writing at home, but try to do the writing immediately.

C. Repeat NJNICA feedback for each story.

D. Ask each writer in the group to repeat the story telling/writing process until they are comfortable writing and receiving feedback. At this point the writing can be done at home.

Remember that each new person added to the group or class needs to be taken through this storytelling/writing process. New group members need to be encouraged to listen for NJNICA feedback, and given a little time to develop NJNICA feedback. With practice and time, the whole group's feedback—and unity—will be all the better for it!

Good luck!

SELECTED READINGS

I. WRITING MODELS

Aiken, Conrad. *Collected Short Stories* (New York, Schocken Books, 1982).
"Silent Snow, Secret Snow" allows us to glimpse a young boy's fascinating and very private world from his point of view.

Bierce, Ambrose. *The Stories and Fables of Ambrose Bierce* (Owings Mills MD, Stemmer House Publishers, 1977).
His stories "Occurence at Owl Creek Bridge," "The Boarded Window," and "One of the Missing," provide us with superbly shocking, unpredictable, mind teasing endings.

Campbell, Joseph. *Hero with a Thousand Faces* (Princeton University Press, 1973). *The Masks of God* (New York, Viking Press, 1970).
The path of the "hero" in all of us is traced through quests and temptations, weaving its way through virtually all of the world's mythologies and religions.

Clurman, Harold. *On Directing* (New York, Macmillan, 1983)
A director and founder of the Group Theater as well as a critic, Clurman gives the reader insights into finding the spine of a dramatic work.

Doctorow, E. L. *World's Fair* (New York, Fawcett Crest, 1985).
Doctorow's novel, which displays a number of techniques of life writing, chronicles the events and experiences of his fictional hero's life.

Dostoevski, Feodor. *Crime and Punishment* (New York, Bantam Books, 1982).
The author interweaves first person narrative, dialogue and inner monologue in this classic story of risk-taking, crime and conscience.

Dreiser, Theodore. *Short Stories of Theodore Dreiser* (New York, Thomas Crowell, 1974).
The narrator's voice in a Dreiser story is often clumsy and intrusive, a legacy of the nineteenth century, yet the stories are well worked out, often gripping and ironic.

Hemingway, Ernest. *Collected Short Stories* (Charles Scribners Sons, 1938).
Hemingway's narrator remains as discreet and inconspicuous as Dreiser's is heavy-handed. The author makes his points dramatically through dialogue and occasional inner monologue.

Ibsen, Henrik. *Collected Plays* (Garden City, New York, Doubleday Books, 1960).
The plot structure and the problems Ibsen sets for his characters and the qualities he gives them make his plays forever interesting.

Lang, Fritz. *M*—Classic Film Scripts, a series (London, Lorrimer Publishing, 1973).
In M, we experience the forcefulness of the pursuers, including the protagonist's own conscience, from the point of view of the criminal pursued.

Miller, Arthur. *Death of a Salesman* (New York, Viking Press, 1959).
The struggle of a character to achieve a goal and the way he pursues it when he can't have what he really wants gives Miller's play dignity and meaning.

Orwell, George. *Collected Essays* (New York, Doubleday, 1957).
"Shooting an Elephant" is classic autobiographical writing— crisp narrative storytelling, a clear view of the objective world facing the writer, physical action, and reflection on the meaning of the actions one takes.

Pirandello, Luigi. *Plays* (Harmondsworth, Middlesex, England, Penguin Books, 1962).
Pirandello's plays bring us into a series of delightfully separate worlds in which each character is convinced his view of the "real world" is correct and each character manages to convince us he is correct.

Stanislavski, Constantin. *The Actor Prepares* (New York, Theater Arts Books, 1970).
The roots of many life-story writing techniques including memory recall, emotion surrounding objects and facts, characters' goals and adjustments, spine, active imagination, and telling a story moment to moment can be found in Stanislavski's work as interpreted by Lee Strasberg and Jack Garfein.

II. LIFE STAGES

Birren, James E., and Schaie, K. Warner. *Handbook of the Psychology of Aging* (New York, Van Nostrand Reinhold Company Inc., 1985).

Erikson, Erik. *The Life Cycle Completed* (New York, Norton, 1982).

Gribben, K., Schaie, K. W., and Parham, I. A. "Complexity of Lifestyle and Maintenance of Intellectual Abilities." *Journal of Social Issues* 365:47-61, 1980.

Schaie, K. W., and Willis, S. L. "Lifespan Development." *Encyclopedia of Educational Research* (New York, Macmillan,1982).

To order, please see last page

ORDER FORM

10% DISCOUNT on orders of $20 or more —
20% DISCOUNT on orders of $50 or more —
30% DISCOUNT on orders of $250 or more —
On cost of books for fully prepaid orders

NAME

ADDRESS

CITY   STATE

ZIP   COUNTRY

TITLE	QTY	PRICE	TOTAL
Paul's Awakening	@	$6.95	
Intrance	@	$9.95	
Not Another Diet Book	@	$15.95	
Believe Me, Doctor—I'm Really Sick	@	$6.95	
The Enabler	@	$6.95	
Everyday Racism	@	$14.95	
Healthy Aging *(paperback)*	@	$11.95	
Healthy Aging *(hard cover)*	@	$17.95	
The Manchilde	@	$14.95	
On the Road to Baghdad	@	$19.95	
Raising Each Other	@	$7.95	
Rastus on Capitol Hill	@	$8.45	
Send information about other Life Story Writing Materials			❑

Shipping costs:
First book: $2.00
($3.00 for Canada)
Each additional
book: $.50 ($.75
for Canada)
For UPS rates and
bulk orders call us
at (714) 624-2277

TOTAL	
Less discount @_____%	( )
TOTAL COST OF BOOKS	
Calif. residents add sales tax	
Shipping & handling	
TOTAL ENCLOSED	
Please pay in U.S. funds only	

❑ Check   ❑ Money Order

Complete and mail to:

Hunter House Inc., Publishers

PO Box 847, Claremont, CA 91711

❑ Check here to receive our book catalog